FIT STARTS IN THE KITCHEN

Photography Credits

Front cover photo: James Patrick

Page iv: Dave Laus

Page 1: Brent Haywood

Page 8: Ralph DeHaan

ACKNOWLEDGMENT

I owe a huge thank you to my husband Justin for his countless taste tests. Not all attempts were successful, and patience was required while working on this book. Many evenings were spent preparing meals, weighing, measuring, calculating, and then photographing prior to eating what would end up being a late dinner. He is my partner, my best friend, and always supports my crazy endeavors.

My daughters Rylee and Dylan, also my toughest critics, were always excited to help with and try my recipes despite their picky palates. I always knew I had hit a home run when they were excited about a recipe. I wish for them to always follow their passion and happiness. I love you both so much.

CONTENTS

ALISSA PARKER IS
Fit in the kitchen

Alissa is an **IFBB** pro figure competitor, certified sports nutrition specialist, coach, wife, and mother of two girls. She has been competing for almost a decade, but she did face struggles along the way. She like most women gained a lot of weight during her first pregnancy. It was getting her body back after when she learned about competing and the world of bodybuilding. After undergoing so many years of dieting, it was becoming apparent that she was dealing with disordered eating. Alissa decided to find ways to eat more freely while still maintaining her physique and not feeling restricted. Her love of food and entertaining has helped her develop these recipes that she cooks not only for herself but for her friends and family on a daily basis.

THE STRUGGLE
My journey

The images we see in fitness magazines of perfectly shaped women and men can be inspiring and discouraging at the same time. While these images portray what looks like the ideal—someone who has it all figured out, the balance of happiness, fitness, and a healthy relationship with food—in many cases, the reality is the complete opposite. Some of the "fittest" people struggle with eating disorders, poor body image, and health problems. As the popularity of fitness is growing there is a greater demand for the fitness industry to speak out and actually preach what we are supposed to be promoting in the first place, and that is HEALTH. I want people to stop beating themselves up and realize that it's not always as it seems.

Like many others, I struggled with body image or body dysmorphia from as young as I can remember. I recall being in preschool and being concerned about my silhouette in a dress and thinking I looked fat. I always thought of myself as being big and bulky, and that I would grow up to be a large woman. In reality, I was very petite. I was under average for height and weight, and was usually the youngest in my grade. For a short period of my young adult life I struggled with anorexia, as much as I hate to admit it, and binge-eating disorder as I got older. It was hard for me to come to terms with this, to admit it was a real problem and to give it up for good. It was my crutch and my Achilles' heel at the same time. As a fitness athlete, I thought I was fine: I was eating healthy, eating a lot, and often. However, with the amount of workouts and long-term dieting, I was having to eat less and work out more to achieve results. It was making me sick. My diet and training was getting too extreme, and I knew I had to make the decision to fix it.

Taking the knowledge and experience I have gained over the years as a competitor and a coach, I was able to turn it around. I started focusing more on having a healthy relationship with food and less on weight and physical appearance. And, what do you know, I actually started to look better, feel better, and gain happiness, not only for me, but for the people around me. I did not do it alone. If you do happen to struggle as I have, there are responsible coaches out there who can help. Even coaches have coaches. We can be too critical in our own heads. If you feel a little lost or confused about nutrition, it's a great investment you can make in yourself. Just make sure you do your research and find someone who is reputable and has the same philosophy you do when it comes to diet and nutrition. I see so many people falling down the same path I was headed. Starting a new diet can feel great at first. The first sign of weight loss is a high. Feeling thin is amazing, but doing it the wrong way does not work in the long run. If I can help even just a few people to achieve a healthier and happier life, all this work will be with it. I want everyone to know you don't have to suffer to be fit. With a little hard work and practice you really can be free from dieting.

THE PROBLEM WITH DIETS
Why they just don't work...

People are always asking me, "What do you eat?," "What should I eat?," or "Can you give me a meal plan?" OK, well, let me just start by saying that not everyone's diet or nutrient intake is the same and following a cookie-cutter diet does not work, especially if you are following a very restrictive meal plan that does not vary. Having a restrictive diet is (a) not fun and (b) not good for you!

Let me tell you why . . .

First of all, if you eat the same food every day or eliminate food groups you will likely have a nutrient deficiency of some sort. It is best to eat a variety of foods.

Restrictive diets may allow you to drop weight quickly, but what happens when you go back to normal eating? You gain weight. If you feel deprived of the foods you love, it will lead to either binging or overindulging when you finally get your hands on that burger you've been craving for a month. I can attest to this firsthand. Being starved and restricted lead me to eat and consume really large quantities of food. Once I started eating everything in moderation, I was able to eliminate cravings for the most part. I was finally released from the hold food had over me. I could finally indulge with one or two bites and be satisfied, unlike before when it took an entire gallon of ice cream.

Lastly, the metabolism, or our body's rate of utilizing energy, is a highly individualized mechanism. Not only is everyone's different, but it can also change based on diet/dieting history, activity level, age, and body composition. As your body changes, so does your metabolic rate, so it's like trying to hit a moving target. A meal plan designed for one person is most likely not right for someone else. Learning how to manage your own diet is important to ensure that you don't end up falling into these dieting traps and fall into a weight loss/gain cycle that just gets harder and harder over time.

ARE YOU REALLY HUNGRY? LEARN YOUR HUNGER CUES

Start to take a good look at your eating habits. When do you feel most hungry? Is it really hunger or something else? Are you an emotional eater? You need to be honest with yourself. I know that I am a bored eater. As soon as I sit down to watch TV I want to eat, hungry or not. Knowing this about myself helps me to deal with it head on. By recognizing your patterns before you are in a situation that causes you to eat when you are not truly hungry is the first step in fighting it off before it arises. Many of us don't truly recognize real hunger cues or feelings of satiety. Eating consciously and consistently will help to regulate your hunger and allow you to truly know when enough is enough.

THE BEST PLAN
The one you can follow long term

Ultimately, the best plan is the one you can follow long term. If your favorite foods just happen to be ones that are off limits, well, then you most likely won't be able to stick to that for very long. This book includes detailed recipes that have allowed me to stick to my caloric and macronutrient requirements, while feeling satisfied. I do not exclude any foods. I do not require my foods to be organic or non-GMO. I do, however, eat a wide variety of foods as well as a high-fiber diet.* I include several lean protein sources and I do try to buy the best-quality ingredients because they just, well, taste better. The point is, whatever is important to you and makes you feel satisfied then that is what you should do. You can use this book as a guide or a source of inspiration for your daily meals. If you want to be vegan, gluten free, Paleo, or just a "clean" eater and that makes you happy (and you can sustain it), then by all means do it! I believe the key is moderation without restriction. Too much of anything can be bad for you, even "healthy" things. Depriving yourself of something you really want can make you want it more in the long run. So have some dessert every day, diet soda, or whatever you crave. As long as you stay within the appropriate amount of calories and macronutrients for your body, you will be on track. If you're sick of dieting like I am, then this is the book for you.

*A note about fiber: getting adequate fiber intake is important for overall health. It helps with digesting and eliminating foods. Fiber adds volume to your meal to keep you feeling fuller longer. It is very low in calories so it's great for keeping you lean. However, it can cause digestive issues like gas and bloating if you up your fiber intake too quickly. If you notice you are having digestive issues, look at your fiber intake. Most Americans eat under well under 30 grams of fiber per day. You may need to slowly increase your intake to keep any digestive stress at bay. Over time the digestive system should get used to a healthy amount of fiber. Digestive enzymes and probiotics can help alleviate some of the tummy trouble.

FLEXIBLE EATING
It's a lifestyle

The word "diet" immediately brings up the thought of deprivation and the idea that there is a time limit on your healthy eating changes. I'd love to just throw this idea out the door. It wasn't until I stopped "dieting" that I found balance. The key to getting healthier and managing a healthy weight is to be consistent, not feel deprived, and enjoy life. A healthy body and mind is important to achieving balance. We all need happiness, right? Balance means we can enjoy everything in moderation. I love to cook up foods with lots of flavor that allow you to feel full but are low enough in calories so you can enjoy more of the foods you love. Most diets are too strict for people to follow long term, causing people to "fall off the wagon" and regain all the weight they lost if not more. Let's stop the ridiculous dieting, and start eating better for a healthy balanced life that we can actually "live" with long term. Flexible eating is a minimally invasive approach to make your goal, whether its losing weight, gaining muscle, or maintaining, easy to adjust and adhere to.

I am a foodie at heart. There aren't enough meals in a day to waste one on something that tastes bland and boring. Even when I am eating fewer calories for a competition or photo shoot, there is no reason to eat foods I don't enjoy. When I was a kid my family wasn't much into cooking. I had to learn on my own how to prepare and enjoy food (especially vegetables). It took a lot of experimentation and trying new foods to learn to enjoy new flavors. I am not a professional chef. I used to joke that I was professional dieter with a love of food. Now I don't consider myself on a diet at all. Traditional diets just didn't work for me, at least not to stick to long term. Over the years I have learned how to have my cake and eat it too, literally! I have developed a healthier relationship with food and I'm much healthier and happier. Cooking your own food at home is a great way to ensure you get quality ingredients and control what you put into your body. It is a great skill to teach your kids and a gift you can pass on to them by setting a good example.

Even if you're a busy parent or have a full-time office job you can still be on the road to a fitter and healthier you. In this book I have compiled my favorite healthy recipes that will help you get started on the right path. Don't think of it as a "diet" but as a way to incorporate some healthy recipes into your arsenal that can keep you satisfied and trim your waistline. It may take some planning, but like all things it gets easier over time. Life happens and we need our eating habits to be able to adapt to the changes in our daily life without it derailing our efforts to be healthy and happy.

THE BASICS
What really matters when it comes to a flexible style of eating

I find that clients who have followed strict meal plans in the past have a harder time understanding this concept. There are no magical foods that make you lean. If you eat anything excessively including vegetables, or anything for that matter, you can still gain body fat if you are going over in calories. Understanding how flexible dieting works is important to your success in terms of body composition and your mental state before, during, and after a diet. The common misconception of flexible eating or If It Fit Your Macros (IIFYM) is that it is a junk food diet. While you can work in the occasional junk food, it is still difficult to feel full enough on junk food alone. Eating higher-volume foods like lean proteins, whole grains, and vegetables will keep you healthy and feeling full enough to stick to your goals.

First, consistency is most important. As long as you hit your target each day you will be on track. You can eat what you want to eat, but you need to hit your numbers. Figure out what works for you, and then make your diet fit that. For example, I'm not usually too hungry in the mornings, so I eat a very light breakfast. I prefer to eat more later in the day so I save most of my calories for then. If I were to eat a big breakfast I would struggle the rest of the day because I would still be hungry and probably end up overeating overall for my daily allowance.

Meal timing, while somewhat important, isn't as critical as focusing on overall consistency for a 24-hour period. Ideally, in order to build muscle you would want protein about four or five times per day about four hours apart. It is not as important for metabolism, as previously thought, to eat several small meals. So the point here is find what works for you. If it works for you and your lifestyle, you will be able to adhere to it for the long term.

Food choices are up to you—that's what is great about this. If you crave something, have it; just fit it into your day. When calories or total macros are low, you have less leeway in terms of food choices. I created all of my recipes to be very "macro friendly" so many are low in fat and low in carbs. If you absolutely love eating whole eggs rather than egg whites or full fat cheese or bacon, for example, just find a way to make those foods fit into your macro nutrient requirements. You do need to keep in mind that micronutrients and fiber are important so eating vegetables and "healthy" or "clean" foods is still important for health. Since vegetables are low in calories, you can eat a lot of volume and keep your belly full.

When life gets in the way, you may think it's the time to hold off on your nutritional goals and get back on track after. With this style of eating you don't need to do that. When I travel, for example, I will try my best to plan ahead. I can usually go on vacation and not gain any weight. In order to be consistent overall, I will eat light during the day and enjoy a nice dinner out. I may not choose the most indulgent item on the menu, but I will enjoy a reasonable dinner and basically eat whatever I want. The point is to find what will work for you and your life on any given day.

FIT STARTS IN THE KITCHEN

THERE IS NO MAGIC PILL ...

Stop looking for the next supplement or fad diet to change your life. There is no magic pill when it comes to having a fit and healthy body.

You have to eat mindfully and engage in some kind of **physical activity**.

Resistance training is a great way to increase lean body mass and metabolic rate, so you can actually eat more. Being fit starts in the kitchen. Fueling your body with the right food to maximize your efforts in the gym will start you on the right path to a balanced and healthy mind and body.

I have designed a majority of my recipes to be low in carbs and fats. I can eat these recipes even when I need to get my body to its absolute leanest. If your carb and fat intake needs to be higher it's always easy to add those to your meals.

To help you come up with a plan that is customized for your individual body and activity level, I have some tips to help you.

HOW MUCH SHOULD I EAT?

DETERMINING HOW MUCH TO EAT PER DAY IS DETERMINED BY SEVERAL FACTORS

- dieting history
- current nutritional intake
- goals (weight loss, building muscle, maintenance)
- activity level

WHAT ARE MACROS?

Macros (short for macronutrients) are protein, carbohydrates, fats, and fiber.

- Protein—4 calories per gram
- Carbohydrates—4 calories per gram
- Fats—9 calories per gram
- Fiber—0-2 calories per gram
- *Alcohol—7 calories per gram

Alcohol is not a macronutrient, but it has to be considered when looking at caloric intake. It is pretty high in calories (almost as much as fat). If alcohol is consumed regularly it could be one of the reasons you're not reaching your goals. It also has none of the nutritional benefits of the macronutrients.

TRYING TO HIT A MOVING TARGET

The metabolism is a tricky thing. If someone has been dieting for a very long time or has had only minimal breaks between diets, their maintenance calories may be quite low. The reason for this is that the metabolism will slow down in periods of starvation in order to keep the body from starving to death. It is a survival mechanism. It also works the other way: if someone has a long period of overfeeding, the metabolism will increase to maintain balance. Finding the right amount of calories is highly individual. Cookie-cutter diets do not work for this reason. By tracking your macronutrient intake you can easily make adjustments to achieve your goals.

FIRST THINGS FIRST

Start out by tracking your intake for a few days. There are several apps that can help you do this easily. Do not change your eating habits at this point. It is important to get a baseline for what you eat normally for maintenance to see what direction you need to move in order to reach your goals.

You will want to track the macros you currently eat. This will allow you to see a clear picture of how you are eating and what your body is used to. If you already know what your macronutrient intake is you can skip this step.

For example, if you are currently eating 2,000 calories per day and maintaining your weight, only a small decrease or increase will move you in the right direction toward your goals. Creating a deficit of 500 calories per day would theoretically allow you to lose one pound per week.

START WITH PROTEIN INTAKE AND THE REST WILL FOLLOW

So you tracked your food for a few days. Now you can see about how many calories you consume to maintain your weight. The next step is to figure out your protein requirement. Protein is important because it allows us to maintain muscle. It is also considered thermogenic. This simply means it burns calories just to digest it. Protein intake can be determined by multiplying your weight by .8 or 1. (1 if you are active). If you are extremely overweight, calculate protein by using your goal weight. Once you calculate your protein intake the remaining calories will be from carbohydrates, fiber, and fats. Fiber is required to keep you healthy, and in general the intake should be around 30 grams per day.

For example, if you weigh 180 pounds and require 2,000 calories per day as determined by your tracking, your daily intake may look like this:

- Protein 180 g = 720 calories
- Carbs 330 g = 1,320 calories
- Fats 60 g = 540 calories
- Fiber 30g = 60 calories

Carb and fat grams can be allocated however you wish, but fats shouldn't be lower than 30 grams.

The daily total adds up to 2,000 calories. If your goal is to lose weight, Leave the protein and fiber intake the same and slowly decrease the number of carbs and fats from your diet. The KEY is to do this **SLOWLY**. You may only need to take out a few grams of carbs and a gram or two of fat to see the scale move in the right direction. You don't need to kill a fly with a hand grenade, just as you don't need to starve yourself right out of the gate when starting a weight-loss plan. If you start too aggressively too soon, you have nowhere to move if things start to stall. Start with a small adjustment. When you feel like you are stuck, make another small adjustment to get things moving again. Trying to cut out more to lose weight faster does not work in the long run, so be patient and go slow.

For help with calculating macros and to find training plans, visit FITSTARTSINTHEKITCHEN.COM.

ACTIVITY LEVEL

Adjustments will need to be made based on your activity level. If you are starting out a rigorous new workout routine you may need to add some calories or at least keep your macronutrient intake the same to lose fat. Just like your diet, your workouts need to be customized for your personal level of fitness. The exact same principals apply here as well as explained earlier. If you don't currently do any physical activity, then starting a high-intensity protocol for lifting will be overkill and most likely lead to injury or burnout. It's about finding a plan that is right for you and your fitness level. As you get more physically fit you can make changes to increase your intensity slowly. This gives you wiggle room, the ability to make changes as you start to adapt.

MEAL PLANS
Some people just do better with a set plan

Some people really like the idea of having a meal plan to follow. When you have no time to calculate on a daily basis, meals need to be made in advance; trying to figure them out causes stress. I've heard a lot of reasons why flexible dieting scares people. That's totally fine. If you're a meal-planning person, than create one for yourself. Take a little time to plan your meals ahead of time, make sure it all fits, and then you can prep ahead and eat without thinking. Making meal plans is not as hard as it seems. Nutritional needs vary from person to person, so pulling up a cookie-cutter plan from the Internet or a magazine is not ideal.

To create a meal plan you can use my recipes as a guide or use the tracking apps to select portion sizes for meals you frequently eat. For some clients I have found this to be a helpful way to get started if it's very new. Then from your meal plan you can begin to make substitutions which will make you better at tracking.

MEAL TIMING
When to eat what, and why it's important

OK, let me start of by saying once again, consistency is key. Recent studies have shown that eating frequently like many diets claim really doesn't make much difference in terms of weight loss, and eating proteins too close together is not as beneficial as having the meals spread a little further apart. So, while **hitting your numbers overall for a day** is the main goal, there are certain instances when meal timing may be something to consider when planning your meals. If you exercise, which you should, you will want to make sure you have enough fuel to perform and recover from your workouts. Fasted cardio is a thing of the past. If you like it and it's the only way to get cardio in, then it's better than nothing, but you definitely don't need to starve yourself before hitting the treadmill. You also want to make sure you get enough protein throughout the day; about four or five servings spread out is ideal. Otherwise, focus on hitting a daily total, especially in the beginning. Don't get hung up on the tiny details.

HOW TO TRACK YOUR MACROS
Once you establish how much to eat, you need to easily find a way to track it.

There are several apps you can use to track your macros. Here are a few, but there are others so find one that is easy for you to navigate.

- Macro Tracker
- My Macros +
- Calorie Counter
- My Fitness Pal

You can set your goal for your daily macros and enter food directly from one of these data bases. I prefer having it on my phone because it is always with me and I can access it anywhere. You can also log your own foods or recipes into the data base and store them for easy access. I will also enter nutritional data from restaurants I eat at frequently that have healthy options. It makes tracking easy when dining out with friends and you can plan ahead.

> **TIP**: if you're in a rush, keep a pad of paper and a pen next to your kitchen scale to write down measurements as you add to your plate. Then log it later.

When you track the foods that you eat, enter all of the macros for that food. For example, a 3 oz. boneless skinless chicken breast is 138 calories, 2.97g fat, 0g carbs, and 26 g protein. It is a protein but also has a small amount of fat.

If you start to run out of carbs and still need protein and fat, meats are a good choice. Egg whites are a good option if you don't want fat or carbs.

You have to get creative in selecting foods to fill in the gaps. With practice this gets much easier. Most of my recipes are low in carbs and fats, so they are macro-friendly for even the strictest times; however, adding a carb as a side dish or dessert is easy,

and the same goes for fat. If you need more fats you can also add things like avocado, nuts, oils, cheese, or fattier cuts of meat.

You will want to know what your overall calories should look like for a typical day in addition to the macros you set for yourself. This will come in handy when things go awry. For example, if you have alcohol you need to subtract that from you carbs and fats for the day. Try to keep protein consistent, but subtract calories from the carbs and fats in any ratio that works best for you that day. Another scenario that this would be helpful for would be if you eat too many carbs you can make up for it in fats, or vice versa, on occasion to keep calories consistent. Calories in and calories out is still a consideration no matter what type of diet you are on. There is simply no diet out there that actually works that allows you to eat an unlimited amount of food.

In the beginning, it may be easier to plan your day in advance until you get used to what your meals should consist of. Remember consistency is key. You don't have to be perfect for this to work, but if you can be close as much as possible that's what counts. As you get better you can track as you go throughout your day.

MEAL PLANNING

Some people work better with a specific meal plan. If this is you, then you can always create a plan for yourself using the macros you set so you don't have to think. You can prep your meals in advance and have them ready to go. You still have the flexibility to change it up whenever you choose to keep it interesting.

DINING OUT

The great thing about eating this way is you still have the flexibility to eat out or go to a party and enjoy life with friends. You just need to plan ahead a bit when you have an event or are eating out. I usually will scope out the menu at restaurants before I go to check to see what I can order that will fit. Many restaurants list the nutrition facts for dishes so it makes it easy to enter it in your food log. If the data are not listed I will do my best to find something similar to compare it to. If I know I am going to a dinner party or an event, I will eat low carb and low fat until that particular meal so that I will keep calories (macros) overall for the day in check.

Things to ask for or look for while dining out:

- When ordering a salad, ask for dressing on the side and fork it on.
- Ask for light or no oil or butter.
- Sauce on the side
- Have meats grilled, steamed, or broiled.
- When ordering a burger or sandwich, you can get it over greens or ask for bun options (brioche is extremely high in fat and calories).
- Order a healthy dish and fill up on that before indulging in other things. If you're already full you will be less likely to overdo the heavier items.
- If you order alcohol with dinner, order water as well to slow down the drinking pace.
- Drinking water while you eat will help you eat less

ESTIMATING

Estimating comes in handy when you are out. You don't need to bring a scale to a restaurant. Once you have been tracking, weighing, and measuring for a while you will get really good at it! If the nutrition facts are not listed at a restaurant, I will simply look at my plate (or take a picture of it so I can track it later) and break down each ingredient by portion size and enter it in. For restaurants you frequent often you can usually save the dish you entered and access it later so you don't have to enter all of the ingredients each time.

The goal here is to get as close as you can. Even nutrition labels are not always 100% accurate, but if we eat mindfully and stay within a reasonable range, we will be on track.

On a final note, you don't have to be at the mercy of tracking for the rest of your life. Once you get in the habit of tracking and knowing what portion sizes should look like you will get better at knowing your body and you can begin practicing intuitive eating.

HOW TO HANDLE ALCOHOL
The best way to indulge and stay on track

As a self-proclaimed foodie, I also like to enjoy adult beverages. I like to indulge in a special craft cocktail or really good wine just like almost everyone else. Let's be realistic here. If you like to have a drink on occasion there is a way to handle it without setting you back. **Alcohol has 7 calories per gram.** There isn't really a designated spot for alcohol as a macronutrient, but because it has calories, and quite a lot, for that matter, we need to address it if we decide to partake. The calories from alcohol should come out of you carbs, fats, or any combination of the two. You can divvy it up however you like as long as you hit your daily total. It won't set you back. Remember the key is consistency and moderation. I you are being conscious of what you put into your mouth, by use of your daily "budgeted" macros it can really help to keep you from just going over the deep end and setting yourself up for failure. Choosing lighter wines, champagne, light beer, and sugar-free mixers is the best way to keep the calories lower. Also a lower alcohol content means fewer calories, so shoot for a lighter option. A spritz is another great option. Half wine, half soda water means half the calories.

Remember to drink in moderation. Drinking to the point of being really drunk can slow you down your metabolism a bit, so don't drink excessively on a regular basis. A trick I use is just to make sure that I hit my protein intake for that day and make sure my total calories are consistent. This way the calories will automatically come out of your carb and fat calories for the day.

FIT TIPS

WEIGHING IN

Remember the scale isn't the only determining factor when it comes to weight loss. If you are weight training, you could be changing your body composition and losing fat and still see the numbers on the scale move up or stay the same. Weighing yourself is a good tool but not the only thing to consider. Going by how your clothes fit and how you feel is also important. If you feel sluggish, tired, and unmotivated to work out, this may be an indication that you are not getting the right amount of fuel. I do weigh myself daily as a tool to keep me accountable. Weight does fluctuate daily, but by tracking this you can begin to see patterns. For example, I usually weigh more the day after I train legs or if I'm getting sick. When I see the slightly higher number on that day I know it is likely water weight, and I don't let it get me down. One the other hand, if I know I've been eating more than I should and the weight is going up, I know I need to be better with self-regulation. Fluctuating a few pounds up or down day to day is normal. But if you look at it over time and it's consistently going up or down then you have a better picture of what is going on.

IT TAKES SOME TRIAL, ERROR, AND PRACTICE

Figuring out your body can be a bit tricky. It may take a few weeks to get it right. Knowing what you are putting into your body will teach you cues to help you reach your goals. Being consistent is far more important than being perfect all the time. If you eat consciously you can actually have your cake and eat it too. You may not want to write down everything you eat, I know, but in the beginning calculating your macros can be really helpful to assess your eating habits. After some time you may not need to. You will have a better idea of portion sizes and be able to figure it out approximately without going through all the trouble. Your intuitive eating skills will become much better. Having a healthy relationship with food can be a learning process if you have struggled in the past. There is no magic pill when it comes to having a fit and healthy body. You have to eat healthfully and engage in some kind of physical activity. Period! Calculating your macros and eating flexibly is the easiest way to achieve and maintain the body you are working toward, healthy for body and mind, as you do not feel the negative effects form extreme dieting and the strain of long-term restriction. I have calculated the macronutrients for all my recipes to help you. Like all things, it takes a bit of practice, so keep at it, and it will be second nature in no time.

WATCH FOR HIDDEN CALORIES

One of the tricks of the trade is knowing how to read a nutrition label. The dietary guidelines are such that if a food is less than 1 gram of any macronutrient it can be listed as 0 grams or 0 calories. This is all dependent on serving size. For example, let's look at spray butter or cooking spray. A 1-second spray is the serving size and that would equal less than 1 gram of fat so it is labeled as 0 calories and 0 grams fat. However, if you read the ingredients list the main ingredient is oil. Oil has fat in it! Many of us use more than the recommended serving size and end up adding way more calories and fat than we think. These products are fine and are great for portion control, but keep in mind that they are not void of calories as the label states. The same holds true for many sugar-free products as well, like gum and sugar substitutes themselves.

WORK SMART
Inefficiency is key

I always find myself trying to explain this concept to my clients, friends, and family when it comes to metabolism. It's all about how well we use up the fuel we put in our bodies.

Unlike a car, ideally, we want to be a gas-guzzling SUV that gets terrible mileage. Why? Well, if you think about it, this means that we don't have to do that much in order to see results. If we trained like a marathon runner and got really efficient at running, then we would start burning fewer calories to run because we would start getting really good at it (becoming more efficient). Muscle is very inefficient in terms of using up calories. This is why having more muscle is metabolically beneficial and why doing hours and hours of cardio is not. If your goal is weight loss, you want to be able to eat as much as possible and do as little as possible in order to drop body fat. Start slow. You need to be able to progress to the next level when you hit a plateau. If you start off too intense you will adapt and have nowhere to go.

REVERSE YOUR DIET
When and how to do it

After a period of calorie reduction or if your calories are already low and you've hit a plateau, this is when you need to consider a reverse diet. A reverse diet is when you slowly reintroduce calories from carbs and fats back into your diet to minimize weight gain. It gives your metabolism the ability to start adapting to more calories. It keeps you from rebounding and packing on the pounds. It will boost your body's ability to burn more and become more inefficient. It is important to do this slowly: five to ten grams of carbs at a time and one to two grams of fat, usually adjusted weekly if you don't see weight gain. Not gaining weight with added calories shows your body has adapted and another slight increase is needed. You do this until you get back to normal maintenance calories and macronutrient intake for your body. I have some clients who eat a lot and it's a good amount of calories; they may not want to add more food at a certain point and that's okay.

Reverse dieting is pretty new and still widely misunderstood. My experience with clients who have been dieting is that they've done well when sticking to the reverse immediately after a completing a diet phase.

This is probably the hardest part of the "diet." When the "diet" (we'll call it diet, but try to think of it as just an adjustment of lower caloric intake for a given period of time) is over, the beginning of the reverse will be only slightly higher in carbs and fats so it may still feel like a "diet" for a bit. It still takes a lot of effort in the very beginning. So when the "diet is "over," it's not really over. Just as you slowly decrease calories for a cutting phase or "diet" you slowly increase them for the reverse. Increases in carbs and fats may be as little as 40-80 calories per week, so take it slow if you want to keep body fat low. Some people respond really well to this, and others take a little longer, but the ability to eat more and more over time is a great reward for all your hard work.

WHAT IF I FAIL?
It's all about how you deal with it...

You may have dieted before, and maybe you've failed. Well, guess what. Everybody fails—it's totally normal. Even the best fail sometimes; it's part of life. If anyone says they don't fail, they're lying. We are perfectly imperfect. It is inevitable. It's how you deal with it that makes the winners win and the losers lose.

The people who love you will still love you, even if you ate too much at a party or snuck into the kids' Halloween candy and ate 15 pieces of it. So why do we beat ourselves up for doing things that sometimes just happen? **Not** learning to deal with these minor setbacks can keep us from making major achievements. Like this for example: you've already eaten something you shouldn't so you just throw in the towel and give up. "Might as well just eat whatever now—I've already screwed up." (This is coming from experience, by the way.) Then comes the guilt, and perhaps a day or a weeks' worth of setbacks. Life happens, and we should be able to enjoy it. I can't even begin to tell you the number of times I have dreaded going out with friends or family. I knew I would either mess up my diet or have to sit around watching everyone eat and drink things I was dying to have. It was a long road for me, but I wouldn't have learned these lessons had I not experienced it. My hope is that by sharing my struggles I can help make it easier for those who follow. There is no need to get sucked into a trap of super restrictive dieting. In the long run it just doesn't work. Health and happiness should come first. A balanced life of fun, as well as hard work that brings you satisfaction, is crucial. Accept your failures, mark them as life experiences that make you stronger, and move on.

I have made it through several dieting and life obstacles, and I continue to work on it all the time. **I fail often**, but I get back on the horse. I go out with friends and eat normal foods within reason. I have a glass or two of wine (maybe more) at least once a week. I have a better relationship with my husband, family, and friends. I am a better mom. I have been able to make the relationships I have with people more of a priority now that I am not doing endless hours of cardio. I finally feel less deprived, happy, and healthy. I work out every day because I love it, and I am conscious of what I feed my body. I have the flexibility to make choices that fit my lifestyle.

MINDSET
How to mentally prepare

I've heard time and time again "I will start Monday" or "This is my last good meal till I hit my goal." In order to be successful for the long term and make a change that will last a lifetime, we need to look at our "diet" differently. Don't think of it as deprivation—that will ultimately send you to craving central. Oftentimes diets interfere with our social lives, missing out on gatherings or outings in order "be good." We only live once, so don't let food get in the way of your fun. You just need to change your mindset. When tracking macros you may be trying to get yourself into a calorie deficit, but you don't need to give up everything in order to get there. Make the foods that are important to you part of your plan so you don't feel deprived. Don't get me wrong—there is some give and take—but it should mean we don't have to give up everything in order to achieve our goals.

Try not to look at this as a diet that you will do for a short period of time; this is really a lifestyle. You can still set small goals, but there shouldn't be an end date. And there really is no reason you can't start as soon as possible, why wait? Starting sooner will just get you that much closer to your goals. Even if you're not perfect, at least you didn't set yourself back by starting the diet with one last really high calorie meal or, even worse, a whole weekend of them. So do something NOW!

WILLPOWER
Who needs it?

Having an iron will only gets you so far. Most diets start out with fiery passion to succeed, but down the road the fire fizzles out. The easiest way to be successful is to not have to exercise your willpower at all. WHAT? No willpower? Yup, that's right, you read that correctly. If we set ourselves up so we don't need to use it, it is so much easier to resist temptations because they won't be staring you in the face. This is where you need to be honest with yourself. Does keeping candy in the house send you to scavenge the cupboards late at night? Well, perhaps that's a good reason to get that stuff out of the house and replace it with a healthier option (I love frozen grapes). Or if you go to a party starving are you more likely to start eating everything in sight? These are the situations you should think about ahead of time to nip it in the bud before it even starts.

Some great tips to get you started:

- Use a smaller dinner plate.
- Don't keep food out on the counter for you to see every time you walk into the kitchen.
- Prepare your plate and bring it to the table.
- Stand further away from the food table at a party.

BODY IMAGE

The grass is always greener on the other side, but is it really?

Poor body image isn't reflective of the body one has. Even people with what most would consider a great physique still struggle. And achieving a fitness goal or weight loss may not even create any real change in how you see yourself. Ultimately, you have to be happy with your body wherever you're at, and that is not always easy.

Body image was something I struggled with for most of my life. I constantly have to remind myself to embrace what I have and live in the moment rather than agonize over a flaw. There were times I was at my leanest, and I couldn't see what was really there. We stand in front of the mirror and immediately our eyes go straight to the trouble spots. Then the negative dialogue starts. We are creating a cycle that trains our brain to see something that is not really there, an exaggerated version of ourselves. We become unwilling to see what others may find attractive. Especially nowadays with social media in our face constantly, we are always comparing ourselves to an unrealistic portrayal of what we should or wish we could look like. Stop comparing yourself to others. It is a waste of time. It seems we usually want what we can't have. Genetics can definitely play a role so, as much as some of us would like to have some parts be a little more this or a little less that, it may just be what makes you the best you. Others may be looking at you the same, wishing they had a body like you, so embrace what your mama gave you. Looking back on times in my life that I was self-conscious, I realize now that I wasn't living and enjoying moments to their fullest. I wasted a lot of time worrying if my butt looked big. Sounds pretty silly, so let it go, there are more important things in life.

A recent study showed people were able to alter their perception of body weight in as little as two minutes. Participants were asked to view images of people that had been digitally manipulated to appear lighter or heavier than they actually were and decide whether these images looked fatter or thinner than "normal."

After 120 seconds of exposure to manipulated thin bodies, the original-sized body images looked abnormally large to participants, while the thinner images were rated as normal. The opposite was also true: exposure to heavier bodies made participants see original body sizes as skinny.[1]

RETRAIN YOUR BRAIN

- Look in the mirror and point out something you like about yourself everyday.
- Set a goal and achieve it—make yourself proud.
- Stop comparing yourself to others.
- Take a break from social media.
- Focus on being healthy and feeling good. Appreciate what your body does for you.
- Remember that friends and family love you regardless of you size or shape.

1 Brooks, K. R., Mond, J. M., Stevenson, R. J., and Stephen, I. D., "Body Image Distortion and Exposure to Extreme Body Types: Contingent Adaptation and Cross Adaptation for Self and Other." *Front. Neurosci.* 10:334 (2016), doi: 10.3389/fnins.2016.00334.

INTUITIVE EATING
You don't have to track forever

Once you have tracked for a while and your body weight is stable and where you want it, this is the time you can start to eat intuitively. What does that mean exactly? Basically it means that you don't really have to track everything to maintain anymore. Tracking for years made me better at recognizing appropriate portion sizes, taught me great habits, and gave me a better understanding of my hunger cues. For example, if I go out to brunch and have a big meal, I may not be hungry for a long time. That meal probably had plenty of calories and I may not need any more food for a while. I don't eat just for the sake of eating. I do try to make sure I get adequate protein intake at about 4 meals per day so I can maintain muscle, but because overall calorie intake is most important for weight management, I don't agonize over meal timing. If you decide to stop tracking, it's a good idea to keep track of your body weight on the scale just to make sure you're maintaining, and not slowly creeping up in weight. People who weigh in daily are more likely to maintain their weight over time than those that don't. Weight fluctuations are normal, but you can tighten up the reins a bit as soon as you start to see the numbers shifting upward before it gets out of control.

The bottom line is that you are still regulating your caloric intake, but instead of weighing, measuring, and tracking, you are listening to your body. Years and years of dieting actually starts to affect the signals your brain sends including feelings of satiety, so it can be really hard to know when you are actually full. While tracking and monitoring intake for a bit, is really helpful to reset and train your brain. Intuitive eating is the ultimate goal. This is the final step in the process and what I hope everyone who reads this book is able to achieve. It is the best feeling to know I am in control.

SUPPLEMENTS
Make sure you get what your body needs

While it's not necessary to take handfuls of vitamins daily, there are a few I think are the most beneficial.

When purchasing vitamins and minerals make sure you check the dosage and make sure it is appropriate for your body. Follow the instructions on the product label. Vitamins A,D,E, and K are fat soluble and are the major ones not to take in mega doses.

- First thing in the morning I like to have some caffeine (in the form of coffee). Check out my hot mocha recipe on page 137. If you choose to take a fat burner like Yohimbine, this would be the time to take it, on an empty stomach.
- After breakfast: Get a good quality Multivitamin & Vitamin C.
- After an evening meal: Multivitamin (if it's a multiple dose formula) calcium and magnesium (helps relax muscles), zinc, vitamin C.
- Pre/during/after weight training workout: Branch-chained amino acid (BCAA) Powder, to be sipped while you work out. BCAAs are the building blocks of protein and they help sustain your muscle throughout your lifting session. They can also be sipped throughout the day between meals. Check my BCAA Gelatin recipe on page 110.

Creatine is great for those interested in muscle building and strength training. It has been shown to increase strength, which can help with gaining muscle over time.

Betaine anhydrous is another supplement that is shown to help with body composition. While it doesn't cause weight loss/gain, it can help lower body fat and increase lean mass. Overall body composition will improve.

- A note about protein powders: Different types of protein powders digest at different rates, so certain ones are better at certain times. A whey protein if eaten alone, for example, is best post workout because it digests most quickly. It is also a high-quality form of protein. You can always add fats to slow down digestion. Casein protein digests slower so it is usually recommended before bed. It can be difficult to digest and can cause GI distress. Many protein powders come as a blend, usually whey, casein, and egg protein. These are sold for a timed release effect and I find are best for cooking with in recipes. I usually have a flavored whey isolate, an unflavored whey isolate, and a blended protein on hand for baking.
- Cooking protein powder is fine; it denatures it just as you would denature chicken after cooking it. It does not affect the nutrient value.
- Glutamine powder helps with recovery and aids in digestion.
- Powdered collagen is good for hair, skin, nails, and joints. I like the powder better than the capsules because the powder is the secret ingredient in my slushy drink recipes on pages 134-136.

FOOD LIST

Any and all foods are OK in moderation, but here's a list of great healthy options

LOW-FAT PROTEINS

- Gelatin
- Protein powder - whey, casein, egg *try to avoid soy and read labels as it is sometimes added to other types of protein powders as a less expensive ingredient
- Fat free or low fat cheese, cottage cheese, cream cheese
- Egg whites
- White fish - tilapia, orange roughy, cod, halibut, red snapper, sea bass, baramundi, swordfish
- Tuna - Ahi, albacore, canned white/light (tuna, swordfish, and orange roughy are higher in mercury, but are fine in moderation)
- Shellfish - crab, lobster, shrimp, scallops, mussels, oysters
- Turkey breast, lean or extra lean ground turkey
- Chicken breast
- Pork tenderloin, pork chops (fat trimmed), extra lean ground pork

SLIGHTLY HIGHER FAT PROTEINS

- 90% or leaner ground beef, top sirloin, fillet mignon, New York strip (fat trimmed) *when buying beef, grass fed beef is leaner that grain fed. Look for cuts that don't have a lot of marbling.
- Salmon - Wild is leaner and better quality than farmed

CARBOHYDRATES

Starches and grains

- yams/sweet potatoes
- red potatoes
- nutrient dense pastas
- whole grain/whole wheat bread
- low carb wraps/tortillas
- corn tortillas
- rice cakes
- beans
- rice (brown, black, or wild)
- quinoa
- corn or popcorn
- oatmeal/ream of wheat
- high fiber low sugar cereal
- Shirataki noodles
- spaghetti squash
- kabocha squash

Fruits

- berries
- bananas
- apples
- grapes
- stone fruits
- dried fruits
- melon
- pineapple
- mango
- kiwi
- cherries
- oranges
- lime/lemons
- coconut

Vegetables (some are technically fruit)

- leafy greens
- broccoli
- cauliflower
- asparagus
- zucchini
- eggplant
- tomatoes
- jicama
- artichokes
- root vegetables
- beets
- celery
- mushrooms
- onion

FATS

- olive oil - There are several infused olive oils on the market that can add flavor and variety to your dishes.
- coconut oil
- nuts
- nut butters
- avocado or avocado oil
- butter
- flax oil/seeds
- seeds - chia, pumpkin, sunflower

CONDIMENTS + SEASONINGS

- sea salt (Salt is important for normal fluid balance. Do not limit unless you have a health issue.)
- pepper
- organic or regular seasoning packets like ranch, French onion, sloppy Joe
- salt free seasonings
- herbs and spices
- mustard - can be very high in sodium
- coconut aminos (lower sodium & gluten free soy sauce alternative)
- Braggs liquid aminos (soy sauce alternative)
- lemon/lime
- vinegar (any)
- Stevia, swerve, or erythritol are my preferred types of sweetener because they are lower in calories. If you find you are not losing weight and are consuming a lot of sugar substitutes, this could be the culprit. They can also cause water retention.

BEVERAGES

- water
- coffee and tea
- diet drinks in moderation

EXTRAS

- Gum and sugar free mints actually do have a small amount of calories but they are okay in moderation. Try to limit them to when you really have a craving. They have calories, so if you're chomping all day it can add up.

FOOD PREP 101
Even if you are super busy, there is always a way

Save the excuses. I know lots of people who manage to get it done with kids, jobs, you name it, myself included. You just have to want it and make it a priority. When it comes to prepping your food, planning is key. Food prep can takes some practice and patience, but trust me, it gets easier. You'll be grateful when it's all done and you have all your meals to go on the ready, especially if you work outside of the house and have a busy schedule. You'll want to plan your meals for the week. Whether you stick to simple preparations or decide to throw in some of the recipes I have created for you, it all starts with a plan. I do not eat the exact same foods every day. Variety is the spice of life. I do, however, try to eat the same amount of macronutrients per day (proteins, carbs, fats, and

fiber). These numbers are determined on an individual basis. It may take a bit of trial and error to figure out what is appropriate for you. The chapter "How Much Should I Eat" will teach you how to get started.

Ideally you'd want to eat between three and five meals per day, with protein at each meal. It is also a good idea to make sure you have fuel for your physical activity, so eating more of your carbohydrates and less fat around your workouts will be beneficial. That would be ideal, but if you can't it is more important to hit your macros. So do what you can. It's all about flexibility here.

First, write out your grocery list and head to the market(s) to pick up your items. You will eventually become an expert on which stores carry which items. You can also ask your grocer if they can order something special for you if you can't find what you're looking for, and everything is available online these days. OK, so you now have bags upon bags of groceries to feed yourself throughout the week, now what? You can start cooking now and avoid the extra step of putting everything away, or you're like me and have 50 other things you need to do first.

Some essential items you'll need to have on hand before you begin are a **food scale**, lots of **baggies in different sizes**, and/or **food storage containers, measuring spoons, and cups**. Weighing out and measuring all your food can be tedious, but at least in the beginning it will ensure you are sticking to correct portion sizes. I have been doing this so long that I usually can pick up the exact amount of food; I do still use my scale and measuring cups, though. It has become a habit, and that's the key to creating these new habits to ensure your success. Always measure your food after its cooked with the exception of oatmeal, popcorn, or rice, which are usually measured before.

Methods of cooking: roasting, baking, steaming, and grilling are all great, easy, and healthy ways to prepare your food. I even use a smoker and sous vide some of my foods; unless you have these already they are more expensive and not necessary—unless you're a foodie like me.

The easiest thing to do, especially during the week, is to plan ahead and have food cooked and ready to go. I usually eat pretty basic on a daily ba-

sis with the exception of my dinner meal. I usually plan my leftover dinners for the next day's lunches or snacks. I have extra proteins and veggies on hand always. This way you can batch cook everything and preportion it all out and have it ready to go during a busy week. The worst thing is to be caught starving with nothing to eat—this is how we set ourselves up for failure. Prepare and plan and you will succeed! I know that when I have already prepared my meals I will eat them because I don't want to waste the food or the time I spent cooking it. You will begin to enjoy the routine and look forward to meals especially as you metabolism gets fired up! If I go out to eat, I always try to scope out the menu online to plan what I will order.

DID YOU KNOW that liquid measuring cups and dry measuring cups can yield different amounts? When measuring dry ingredients scoop and sweep off the excess with a flat utensil. When measuring a liquid, fill the cup to the mark and get down at eye level to make sure the meniscus reaches the desired mark. This is especially important for baking, when ingredients must be quite accurate for a recipe's success. When it comes to counting calories, being slightly off day after day can lead to way more or less calories than desired. If you want to be 100% accurate use the scale. Set your scale to measure in grams. It's the best way to ensure accuracy.

BASIC FOOD PREP
The healthiest way to prepare your food simply

VEGETABLES

You can eat your veggies raw, steamed, grilled, or roasted. Frozen veggies are fine as they are usually frozen at peak freshness. Here are a few of my favorite ways to prepare my veggies.

- Spinach—raw in salad, or I will wilt it in a sauté pan.
- Zucchini—raw, sautéed with a little bit of cooking spray, roasted on a baking sheet with light cooking spray until very crispy, or grilled.
- Broccoli and cauliflower—raw, steamed, roasted.
- Cabbage—raw, finely shredded, sautéed with cooking spray.
- Brussels sprouts—shredded and eaten raw, blanched then roasted on a sheet pan in the oven with just a touch of cooking spray and salt and pepper.
- Asparagus—roasted or grilled, brings out a meatier savory flavor as opposed to steaming, which brings out a grassier flavor.
- Romaine lettuce—raw or grilled.
- Mushrooms—grilled or sautéed with cooking spray. To clean mushrooms, wipe any dirt off with a towel. If washed they will absorb too much water.
- Green beans—I prefer to eat them raw.

MEAT/POULTRY/FISH

- Chicken—roasted, grilled, sauteed, smoked.
- White Fish—pan seared, grilled.
- Salmon and swordfish—Grilled, broiled, or smoked. You can get an inexpensive smoker box for your grill to get smoke flavor without the expense of a smoker grill.
- Shrimp—pan seared, steamed, grilled.
- Beef—season with salt and pepper, grill or sear in a pan over high heat and finish in the oven.

CARBOHYDRATES

- Yams—roasted in the oven at 350 degrees F for an hour if they're not soft yet. I will cover them in the oven with foil, turn off the heat, and let them cook low and slow and keep checking them for doneness. I eat the skins too—that's where all the nutrients are. Since you eat the outside, these might be best to buy organic and make sure you wash and scrub them very well. You can also cut them into fries, but I find if you bake them from a frozen state they actually turn out crispier.
- Oats—steal-cut old-fashioned oats are better than instant. I cook with water in the microwave and measure before I cook them. They can also be milled into flour and used for baking.
- Rice—I usually buy the microwavable varieties to save time and the portions are smaller, but make sure to check the label for added fat. If I make a large batch, I will use a rice cooker.

BREAKFAST

Lemon protein waffles

Pumpkin and chocolate pancakes

Heavenly oatmeal

French toast with orange glaze

Strawberry banana bars

Powered-up muffins

Simple breakfast bars

Cheesy breakfast sandwiches

B.L.T. scramble

SERVE WITH VANILLA GLAZE

- 1 tbsp powdered swerve
- 1/2 tsp vanilla bean paste
- 1/2 tbsp water

LEMON PROTEIN WAFFLES

176 calories, 1 g fat, 10 g carbs, 30 g protein, 2 g fiber   2 servings

DRY INGREDIENTS:

- 1 scoop whey protein (vanilla or unflavored)
- 1 tsp vanilla
- 1/2 cup garbanzo bean flour
- 1/2 tsp baking powder
- 1/2 tsp baking soda
- 1/4 tsp salt

WET INGREDIENTS:

- 1 individual container of nonfat Greek yogurt (170 g)
- 2 egg whites (65 g)
- 1 tsp vanilla
- 1 lemon zest and the juice (2 lemons if they are small)

DIRECTIONS:

In a bowl, stir together all of the ingredients. Place in a preheated waffle iron and cook on a medium setting.

PUMPKIN AND CHOCOLATE PANCAKES

206 calories, 32 g protein, 10 g carbs, 5g fat, 2.5g fiber   1 serving

The protein powder used has 120 calories, 24 g protein, 3 g carbs, 2 g fat

INGREDIENTS:

- 2 egg whites or 65 g
- 1 scoop or 36 g protein powder (I have used vanilla, peanut butter, and pancake flavors)
- 1/4 cup or 63 g of pureed canned pumpkin, unsweetened
- 1/2 square or 8 g 85–100% cacao chocolate, chopped
- 2 stevia packets
- 1/2 tsp vanilla
- 1 tsp pumpkin pie spice
- 1/4 cup calorie-free syrup to serve alongside

DIRECTIONS:

Combine all ingredients except for syrup in a small mixing bowl. Cook in a preheated skillet over medium heat with a small amount of cooking spray. It's ready to flip when you see some bubbles forming and the edges look crisp. Cook for about 1 more minute. Serve with calorie-free syrup.

If you use a whey isolate protein powder, be careful not to overcook. It will become rubbery. Protein blends will have a fluffier texture.

AN EXCELLENT SOURCE of antioxidants from the pumpkin and dark chocolate.

Fantastic around the holidays for a guilt-free festive treat.

This also makes a great low-carb high-protein-filled dessert.

Try it in the waffle iron!

DESSERT FOR BREAKFAST— WHY NOT?

This is a super fast breakfast great for those busy mornings.

HEAVENLY OATMEAL

347 calories, 35.3 g protein, 30.33 g carb, 11 g fat, 5.7 g fiber   1 serving

INGREDIENTS:

- 1/3 cup old-fashioned oats, dry measure
- 2/3 cup water
- 1 scoop chocolate whey protein powder
- 1 tbsp unsweetened shredded coconut
- 1 tsp stevia chocolate chips
- pinch sea salt

DIRECTIONS:

Combine the oats and water and cook. I prepare mine in the microwave. After cooking the oats mix in the protein powder and top with the coconut and chocolate chips and sprinkle with a pinch of sea salt.

FRENCH TOAST WITH ORANGE GLAZE

149 calories, 13 g protein, 26 g carbs, 1 g fat, 7 g fiber

1 serving (2 slices)

INGREDIENTS:

- 2 egg whites, or 65 g
- 1/2 tsp vanilla paste
- 1/4 tsp cinnamon
- pinch of sea salt
- 45 g or 2 slices of 45-calorie whole grain bread

GLAZE INGREDIENTS:

- 17g or 1 tbsp sugar-free orange marmalade
- 1 tbsp water

DIRECTIONS:

Preheat a nonstick skillet over medium heat. While heating, mix egg, vanilla, cinnamon, and sea salt. Soak both pieces of bread in the mixture. When the pan is hot lightly coat with cooking spray. Place toasts on the skillet, pour any remaining egg mixture over the top, and cook until golden brown, about three or four minutes on the first side. While the first side is cooking combine the ingredients for the glaze in a small bowl and reserve for serving. Once the French toast is ready to flip cook another minute or two until golden brown. Pour the glaze mixture over and serve.

DELICIOUS, QUICK, AND EASY

Look for bread that is low in calories and high in fiber. I found one that has 45 calories per slice, and even the kids like it.

POWERED-UP MUFFINS

1 MUFFIN: 51 Calories, 3.4g protein, 10g carb, 1g fat, 10g fiber   18 muffins

WET INGREDIENTS:

- 1 cup shredded carrots
- 1 medium zucchini, shredded
- 2 egg whites
- 1 tsp vanilla
- 1 tbsp chia seeds
- 1/3 cup raisins
- 1 tsp fresh ginger
- 1 cup crushed pineapple
- 1/3 cup swerve (77 g)

DRY INGREDIENTS:

- 1 cup carb quick
- 1/2 tsp baking powder
- 1 tsp baking soda
- 1 tsp cinnamon
- 1/2 tsp nutmeg
- 1/4 tsp salt
- 1/2 cup whey protein powder (unflavored)
- 1/2 cup oats

DIRECTIONS:

Preheat the oven to 350 degrees F. You will need a muffin pan and muffin liners. This recipe makes 18 muffins. In a large bowl combine all of the wet ingredients and set aside. In another smaller bowl combine the dry ingredients and mix. Add the dry to the wet ingredients and stir until combined. Using an ice cream scoop fill each muffin cup, and bake for 12–14 minutes, until a toothpick comes out clean from the center of a muffin.

Allow to cool and serve alone or with cream cheese icing on page 119.

THESE ARE GREAT WITH CREAM CHEESE FROSTING ON PAGE 119, or cut in half with a scoop of light ice-cream for healthy ice cream sandwich.

You can use unflavored, vanilla, or cinnamon-flavored protein powder, but the flavor may vary. The nutrition fact may vary slightly depending on the protein powder you use.

A GREAT WAY to get protein packed snack or breakfast on the go. You can add other fruits, different flavors of protein, cocoa powder, or chocolate chips to change up the flavor.

Bake ahead and preportion for mornings on the go.

STRAWBERRY BANANA BARS
3 BARS PER SERVING: 200 calories, 21 g protein, 21 g carb, 4 g fat, 2g fiber

9 bars total

INGREDIENTS:

- 100 g or 1 medium banana, mashed
- 140 g or 4 egg whites
- 1 whole egg (large or 55 g)
- 1 tsp vanilla extract or vanilla bean paste
- 2 scoops or 70 g whey protein powder (I used peanut butter flavor)
- 2 tbsp swerve sweetener
- 1/4 tsp sea salt
- 1/2 cup old-fashioned oats
- 1/2 cup or 7 g roughly chopped freeze-dried strawberries

DIRECTIONS:

Preheat the oven to 350 degrees F. Lightly coat a 9 x 5 baking pan with cooking spray and set aside.

Mash the banana in a medium-sized bowl. Add eggs and blend with a hand blender until well combined and light and fluffy. Add the vanilla, protein powder, sea salt, and sweetener, and blend until combined.

Stir in the oats and strawberries. Pour into greased pan and bake for 14–18 minutes. Keep an eye on it. Overbaking whey protein will make them rubbery.

SIMPLE BREAKFAST BARS

140 calories, 13.8 g protein, 17 g carbs, 1.5 g fat, 3.35 g fiber · · · · · · · · 4 servings

INGREDIENTS:

- 12 egg whites, or 400 g
- 1 cup dry old-fashioned oats
- 1 tbsp raw mesquite powder (optional)
- 1 tsp vanilla or vanilla bean paste
- 1 tsp cinnamon
- pinch sea salt
- 2 tbsp swerve sweetener
- 1/4 cup calorie-free maple syrup

DIRECTIONS:

Preheat oven to 350 degrees F. Lightly coat a 9 x 5 baking pan with cooking spray and set aside.

Combine all ingredients EXCEPT FOR THE OATS in a bowl and box using a hand blender, regular blender, or hand mixer. Beat until it becomes light and fluffy. Stir in the oats and pour into the baking dish.

Bake for about 20 minutes, until the center is firm. Slice into squares and serve with sugar-free syrup or sprinkle with sea salt and stevia or even add a little cinnamon. Store the remaining bars in the fridge for breakfast on the go for the next few days.

ARE YOU SICK OF EGG WHITES AND OATMEAL?
Try this recipe!

Raw mesquite powder adds a smoky flavor and it's rich in minerals, fiber, magnesium, and calcium. Find it at your local health food store or online.

A SWEET AND SAVORY meal that's quick and easy.

When buying prepackaged deli meats you can find organic or nitrate-free varieties. Look for one that is low in fat.

CHEESY BREAKFAST SANDWICHES
225 calories, 22.8 g protein, 20 g carbs, 3.5 g fat, 3.35 g fiber   1 serving

INGREDIENTS:

- 1 serving of simple breakfast bars (recipe on page 34)
- 40 g or 2 slices of prepackaged low-fat ham or turkey
- 1 slice fat-free cheese
- calorie-free maple syrup, powdered swerve, sugar-free jam or ketchup to serve on the side

DIRECTIONS:

Start by cutting one serving of the simple breakfast bars on the previous page into even pieces. This will be the bread for your sandwich. Place two slices of ham or turkey and top with nonfat cheese. Sprinkle with powdered stevia, and serve with calorie-free maple syrup and/or sugar-free ketchup.

B.L.T. SCRAMBLE

251 calories, 28 g protein, 14.6 g carb, 9 g fat, 4 g fiber   1 serving

INGREDIENTS:

- 130 g egg white, raw
- 70 g tomato, diced
- 1 slice turkey bacon, sliced into lardons
- 25 g lettuce, romaine
- 1/4 tsp sea salt
- 1 whole extra large or jumbo egg, about 60 g
- 1 slice of 45 calorie whole grain bread

DIRECTIONS:

In a preheated pan, cook turkey bacon and set aside. In the same pan scramble the egg whites. Plate the egg whites for serving and before adding the other ingredients, crack one egg in the hot pan over medium heat lightly coated with cooking spray. Place a lid over the pan and let cook just until the whites become solid, leaving the yolk runny, be careful not to overcook. You'll have to keep a close eye on it. While the egg is cooking, pop a piece of bread in the toaster for your "croutons." Then top the egg whites with sea salt, the cooked bacon, lettuce, and tomato. As soon and the whole egg is cooked, put it on the egg whites. Cut the toast into cubes and sprinkle over the top and serve.

APPETIZERS

I ALWAYS MAKE THIS FOR A PARTY.
I serve it alone in a chilled dish or with diced avocado, wasabi cream, and either wonton chips or shells so people can make their own tacos.

AHI POKE

150 calories, 28 g protein, 4.7 g carb, 1.2 g fat, <1 g fiber
Makes eight - 4 oz. portions

INGREDIENTS:

- 2 lbs fresh sashimi grade ahi tuna
- 70 g or 1 small or 1/2 large onion, julienne cut (Maui onion or other sweet onion)
- Marinade:
- 30 g or 2–3 scallions, sliced on a bias whites and greens
- 1/2 teaspoon freshly grated fresh ginger (I keep fresh ginger peeled and in the freezer, so I always have it on hand)
- 3 finely diced garlic cloves
- 1/2 cup coconut aminos
- 1 teaspoon sesame oil
- 1/2 teaspoon red pepper flakes
- 1 teaspoon Sriracha
- 1 teaspoon sea salt

DIRECTIONS:

Cut Ahi into at least 1/2" cubes. Make sure to keep it cold: put it back in the fridge while you get the other ingredients together.

Combine all other ingredients in a large glass bowl and refrigerate for at least 30 minutes before adding the fish. Before serving toss all ingredients together. Serve with a lime wedge on the side

CHINESE CHICKEN SKEWERS

PER SKEWER + DIPPING SAUCE:
80 calories, 13 g protein, 3.5 g carb, <1 g fat, <1 g fiber   Makes 16 skewers

INGREDIENTS:

- 2 lbs boneless skinless chicken breasts
- Chinese spice blend:
- 8 star anise
- 2 tsp Szechwan peppercorns
- 1 tbsp fennel seeds
- 1/2 tsp cloves
- 2 cinnamon sticks or 1 tbsp ground cinnamon
- 1 tbsp brown sugar
- 1 tbsp sugar substitute (I like swerve)
- 1 tsp sea salt
- 2 tsp garlic powder
- 2 tsp ground ginger
- 2 tsp turmeric
- 1/3 cup coconut aminos

DIPPING SAUCE:

- 1/2 cup coconut aminos
- juice from 1/2 lemon (a juicy one)
- 1 tsp sesame oil
- 1 tsp Sriracha

DIRECTIONS:

Combine star anise, peppercorns, fennel seeds, cloves, and cinnamon sticks (if using ground cinnamon do not add yet) in a sauté pan on medium heat. Toast the spices for a minute until fragrant. Add the spices to a spice grinder, grind to a fine powder. Add the sugars, salt, and additional ground spices.

Slice chicken breasts lengthwise into 1-inch strips (helps if it's slightly frozen—just pop fresh chicken breast in the freezer for 30 minutes). Coat with some of the spice powder blend. Then pour over the soy or soy sauce alternative and make sure the chicken is coated. If you have time allow to marinate for a few hours.

Push chicken onto skewers that have been soaked for about 30 minutes.

Cook on a grill for about 4-5 minutes per side, until the internal temperature reaches 165 degrees F.

To make the dipping sauce, just combine all ingredients and serve alongside the chicken.

PORTION-CONTROLLED skewers make a great appetizer or snack. Make it a main dish by using the spice mixture on a small chicken breast and serve with veggies or a salad.

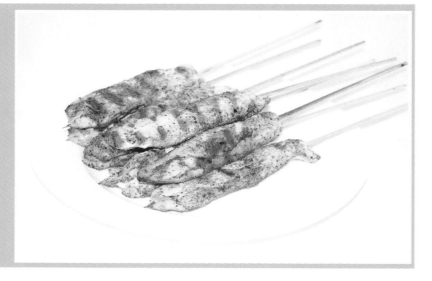

SERVE ALONGSIDE
sweet chili and peanut sauce
recipes on page 103.

Keep them wrapped
individually in plastic wrap or
foil so they don't stick together.
A great make-ahead snack.

SUMMER ROLLS
96 calories, 4 g protein, 20 g carbs, <1 g fat, 3.5 g fiber per roll   Makes 6 rolls

INGREDIENTS:

- 6 9" rice paper wraps
- 6 oz. carrots, julienne
- butter lettuce leaves
- 6 oz. jicama
- 6 oz. zucchini, julienne
- 12 oz. firm or extra firm tofu
- coconut aminos
- 6 whole basil leaves, 1 per roll

DIRECTIONS:

Heat a skillet over medium high heat. Slice tofu into 1/2" strips. Pour a little coconut aminos over the tofu and sear in the pan with a light spray of cooking spray. Remove from heat. Fill a shallow bowl, large enough to hold the rice paper, with hot tap water. Get your rolling station ready with veggies diced and tofu. Soak one rice paper wrap for about 15 seconds till it softens. Place on a towel and begin to fill with your ingredients. Take two lettuce leaves, a few pieces of the zucchini, jicama, some carrots, and 1 strip of tofu, and roll like a burrito tightly. Just before you finish rolling it up place a leaf of basil just beneath the rice paper. The sticky rice paper will seal it up.

NO RICE! Using the same ingredients as the summer rolls, this is a low-carb option served alongside coconut aminos instead of soy sauce.

Sashimi grade ahi or seared steak would be great here too.

LOW-CARB SUSHI ROLLS

71 calories, 5 g protein, 11.9 g carbs, <1 g fat, 4.5 g fiber per roll   Makes 6 rolls

INGREDIENTS:

- 6 nori sheets
- 6 oz. carrots, julienne
- butter lettuce leaves
- 6 oz. jicama
- 6 oz. zucchini, julienne
- 12 oz. firm or extra firm tofu
- coconut aminos

DIRECTIONS:

Heat a skillet over medium high heat. Slice tofu into 1/2" strips. Pour a little coconut aminos over the tofu and sear in the pan with a light spray of cooking spray. Remove from heat. Get your rolling station ready with veggies diced and tofu or protein of your choice. Take a sheet of nori and place on a towel and begin to fill with your ingredients. Take two lettuce leaves, a few pieces of the zucchini, jicama, some carrots, and one strip of tofu, and roll using the towel; tightly wrap the roll. Lightly moisten the edge of the roll with water to seal it up. Slice and serve.

TURKEY LARB LETTUCE CUPS

80 calories, 15 g protein, 4.7 g carbs ,<1 g fat, 1 g fiber per serving   8 servings

INGREDIENTS:

- 1 lb extra lean ground turkey
- 1 shallot, sliced
- 1/2 to 1 tbsp chili flakes
- 1/2 tbsp fish sauce
- lime juice, 1–2 limes
- 1/2 to 1 whole stevia packet, depending on desired sweetness
- 3–4 green onions, sliced
- hand full of basil leaves (Thai basil if you can find them); you can also use mint or a combination of both
- Lettuce cups for serving

DIRECTIONS:

Brown the turkey and shallots over medium high heat. While that's cooking mix together the chili flakes, fish sauce, lime juice, and stevia. Add to the cooked turkey mixture. Add the sliced green onions and tear up about 20 basil leaves. Toss and serve alongside lettuce cups. A serving size is about 2 oz. of the mixture in the lettuce cup.

LARB IS A THAI DISH
that is traditionally made with pork and is cooked with rice flour. I used extra lean ground turkey and no rice flour to make it ultra light and low calorie, but still with all the flavor.

THESE HARISSA MEATBALLS **ARE GREAT TO SERVE AT A PARTY** as an appetizer or as a main dish. You can substitute beef or turkey, and they're great over steamed spaghetti squash for an entrée.

Make these for a weeknight dinner with leftovers for the next day. I always serve these with a spoonful of cool nonfat Greek yogurt.

HARISSA CHICKEN MEATBALLS

200 calories, 16 g protein, 17.4 g carb, 8.3 g fat, 5.15 g fiber

8 servings, 3 meatballs each + 1/2 cup sauce

FOR THE MEATBALLS:

- 2 lbs extra lean ground chicken
- 2 eggs
- 1/2 cup panko bread crumbs
- 1/2 of the spice blend (below)
- 1/4 cup amaranth seeds (optional)
- 2 tbsp chopped parsley
- 1 tsp onion powder
- 1 tsp garlic powder
- 1 tsp sea salt
- 1 1/2 tbsp ground cumin
- 1/2 tsp ground turmeric

FOR THE SPICE BLEND:

Reserve half of this mix for the meatballs and half for the sauce

- 1/2 to 1 tsp cayenne pepper
- 2 tsp paprika
- 2 1/2 tbsp cinnamon
- 2 tsp crushed red chili pepper
- 2 tsp caraway
- 2 tsp coriander

FOR THE SAUCE:

- 1 tbsp olive oil
- 1/2 cup chopped onion
- 1 clove garlic, minced
- 1 anchovy fillet (optional)
- 1 28-oz. can diced San Marzano tomatoes
- 1/4 cup white vinegar
- reserved portion of spice blend
- 3 tbsp swerve sweetener
- 1 tsp sea salt

- 1 tbsp ground ginger
- 1/4 tsp ground cloves
- 1/4 tsp ground allspice

DIRECTIONS FOR MEATBALLS:

Start by getting all your ingredients ready; there are a lot of spices so make sure you have them on hand. For the spice blend combine all the ingredients in a spice grinder or a clean coffee grinder. Mix until combined. Combine all of the meatball ingredients in a large bowl. Mix thoroughly and form into 18–24 meatballs (about 2 inches in diameter). You can make them smaller so they are bite sized, but adjust the cooking time. Place the meatballs on a parchment-lined sheet pan and bake at 400 degrees F for 15–18 minutes until golden brown.

DIRECTIONS FOR SAUCE:

While the meatballs are baking, heat the oil in a medium saucepan, then add the onions, garlic, and anchovy. The anchovy will dissolve. Cook over medium heat until the onions are soft, but not browned—about 5 minutes. Add the tomatoes, vinegar, and all of the spices and stir until well combined. Cook on medium heat for 15 minutes. When the meatballs are done, add them to the sauce and cover. Simmer the meatballs in the sauce on very low heat for 15 minutes up to a few hours for best results. Add a few tablespoons of water if the sauce gets too thick. Garnish with some fresh chopped parsley or cilantro.

EGG DROP SOUP

50 calories, 6 g protein, 2.2 g carbs, 1.5 g fat, 0 g fiber per cup   Serves 4

INGREDIENTS:

- 1 quart low-sodium fat-free chicken broth
- 1 tbsp coconut aminos or low-sodium soy sauce (if you use coconut aminos, you may need to add salt)
- 1 tbsp rice vinegar
- 1/4 tsp ginger
- 1 tsp Sriracha
- 1–2 scallions, sliced
- 1 egg white
- 1 whole egg

DIRECTIONS:

Add all ingredients except the egg in a saucepan over medium high heat. Let simmer for 5 minutes. Beat the eggs in a container with a pouring lip. Use a fork to stir the soup in a circle. Begin to pour the eggs 1/4 at a time. Stir as the eggs cook and turn into shreds.

A GREAT-TASTING low-calorie soup. Helps you feel full and won't add too many calories, so you can add it to any meal or enjoy as a snack.

Great for entertaining!

I ALWAYS MAKE THESE IN THE FALL.
Great as a snack or a salad topper.

ROASTED PUMPKIN SEEDS

200 calories, 8.4 g protein, 9.4 g carbs, 15.8 g fat, 1.3 g fiber
Per 1/4 cup serving

OPTION 1 INGREDIENTS:

- Raw pumpkin seeds still in the shell
- low-sodium Worcestershire sauce
- salt and pepper

DIRECTIONS:

After scraping the seeds out of your pumpkin or squash, wash off all the slimy stuff. Lay out on a sheet tray over night to dry out. Preheat the oven to 350 degrees F. On a sheet tray lined with foil and cooking spray place seeds in an even layer, spray them lightly with cooking spray, and dash them with a light coating of low-sodium Worcestershire sauce. Salt and pepper and roast in the oven for 15–20 minutes.

OK, THEY'RE NOT ACTUALLY "FRIED."

They're baked, but still hit the spot.

I serve them with fat-free or low-fat ranch dressing.

"FRIED" PICKLES

105 calories, 5 g protein, 17 g carbs, 2 g fat, 2.5 g fiber   4 - 1/2 cup servings

INGREDIENTS:

- 1 jar of sliced dill pickles
- 1/2 cup whole wheat flour
- 1/2 cup panko bread crumbs
- 1 extra large egg, beaten
- salt and pepper
- nonstick cooking spray

DIRECTIONS:

Heat the oven to 400 degree F. Get three small bowls for your breading station. In the first bowl beat the egg. The second bowl is for the flour seasoned with salt and pepper, and the last is for the panko. Take each pickle and start by coating in the flour, then the egg, back in the flour and then to the panko. Place on a baking sheet lightly coated with cooking spray. When you have finished coating all your pickles, lightly spray with cooking spray so they can get golden brown in the oven. Bake about 15 minutes, turning over once.

ZUCCHINI CHIPS

40 calories, 2 g protein, 6 g carb, 1 g fat, 2.6 g fiber   2 servings

INGREDIENTS:

- 4–5 zucchini squash
- cooking spray
- sea salt or other seasoning

DIRECTIONS:

Wash and slice the zucchini on a bias about 1/4 inch thick. If the slices are too thin they will be crispy but won't hold up to a dip. They will shrink a lot after dehydrating or baking. I dehydrate mine on high for a few hours until crispy; you can bake them in a low-heat oven about 250 degrees for a few hours, turning halfway through the cooking time as well if you don't have a dehydrator. I just give them a light coating of cooking spray so the seasoning will stick. Sea salt is my basic go-to, but Cajun seasoning or a sprinkle of ranch or BBQ seasoning would be great too.

LOW CALORIE CHIP

alternative with all the salty crunch of the real thing.

I use a dehydrator, but you can also bake them at 250 degrees.

SALADS

THE ART OF SALAD

How to make a great salad

Have you ever gone out to a restaurant and ordered a salad only to be disappointed when what is set before you is some half-wilted lettuce, a few shreds of carrot, maybe a cherry tomato, and some nasty store-bought vinaigrette? Don't even get me started on the cold chicken. Nothing is more disappointing when dining out. Making a salad delicious is so easy. It doesn't need to be an afterthought or be some boring, bland, rabbit food. When a salad is made well, it can be a delicious and satisfying meal. I love the variety of a good salad with each bite different than the next. When I eat out I look to order a salad if I can find a good one on the menu. I can always ask for the dressing on the side or substitute a vinaigrette rather than a creamy dressing or ask for no cheese or bacon if I'm trying to keep it light. Making sure I try to order an entrée with fewer calories allows me the flexibility to enjoy some bread or even a drink with my meal. I have compiled my tips for ensuring the tastiest of salads with endless possibilities.

First let's think about taste. You tongue can taste sweet, sour, salty, bitter, umami (savory or meaty), and we can't forget about texture. Somewhere on the spectrum of all the main flavors, is another I like to call pungency or "the funk" think blue cheese or onion and garlic. When all of these elements of taste are compiled into one dish we perceive that as a satisfying experience. As with any dish, not just salads, the key is balance and contrast. And, please, never forget to season your greens with salt and pepper!

SWEET:

Adding a sweet element to a salad can really be a nice surprise and great contrast to the other flavors. Some sweet additions to choose from:

- fresh or dried fruits
- corn
- candied nuts
- fruit juice or other sweetener in your vinaigrette

SOUR:

Adding acidity to a salad is easiest with your dressing. Here are a few sour components:

- vinegar from your vinaigrette, or added alone
- lemon/lime juice, zest or both
- Greek yogurt
- pickled vegetables

SALTY:

Salt enhances flavor. Using a good quality salt adds important minerals. There are different types of gourmet salts and each has a slightly different flavor.

- sea salt, Himalayan pink salt, fleur de sal
- soy sauce
- seaweed, wakame, or other sea vegetables
- fish sauce, anchovies, (umami, but also salty)

BITTER:

- grapefruit
- bitter lettuces - arugula, radicchio, frisée, endive, kale

UMAMI:

Foods that add umami flavor may not sound all that great to you, but the addition in the right amount can make all the difference. People will love it and not know why.

- white or black truffles, oil, or in salt
- mushrooms
- fish sauce, anchovies
- meat, chicken, or fish

PUNGENT OR SPICY:

Something with a lot of flavor that can be lightly added to create a pop of flavor and contrast.

- garlic, onions
- strong flavored cheese, blue cheese, goat cheese
- kimchi
- ginger
- horseradish, wasabi
- mustard
- hot peppers

TEXTURE AND TEMPERATURE:

Different textures like crunchy, crisp, creamy, chewy, or soft add a lot of dimension. Just chopping, slicing, or shaving different ingredients can really enhance texture. We also need to take into consideration contrast in temperature. Add warm freshly grilled chicken or roasted veggies to a cool crisp salad.

PICK YOUR GREENS
Or maybe they're not green at all ...

Just because you're making a salad doesn't mean it has to include lettuce, but if you're so inclined here's a great list of lettuce to choose from when you're in need of a salad makeover. When making your own blend of lettuces, try one from each.

- Mild flavored greens—iceberg, romaine, butter, or Boston bib, escarole, mesclun, leaf lettuce
- Hearty or crisp greens—spinach, kale, Swiss chard, cabbage, romaine
- Flavorful, bitter, or peppery greens— arugula, radicchio, endive, frisée, dandelion, bok choy, watercress
- Fresh herbs added to a salad really create a gourmet flavor. Try adding mint, dill, or cilantro.

A SALAD SPINNER
is a great tool to have in the kitchen to thoroughly wash and dry lettuce.

Wet lettuce waters down the dressing and decreases the flavor.

MAKE IT A MEAL
Not everyone is on a low-carb diet

Make it a full meal with a hearty serving of carbohydrates. Pre and post workout is a great time for an additional carb-filled topping.

- fruits
- beans – black, pinto, fava, white, garbanzo
- grains – quinoa, rice, amaranth, farro
- lentils
- roasted or raw and thinly sliced/diced root vegetables like sun chokes, yams, parsnips, beats
- raw or roasted squash like butternut, kabocha

VINAIGRETTE, THE FORMULA
Never buy store-bought salad dressing again!

VINEGAR/ACID:
If you like less acidity you can add some water
- apple cider, rice, white wine, sherry, red wine, balsamic, lemon juice, lime juice

OIL/FAT:
- olive oil, infused oils, macadamia nut oil, canola oil
- bacon fat, coconut oil (solid at room temp so need to be kept warm)
- yogurt or miso
- flavored oil like sesame oil, chili oil. They can be strong and should be used sparingly for flavor.

EMULSIFIER:
The emulsifier allows the oil and vinegar to mix.
- mustard
- honey, maple syrup, agave, coconut nectar
- egg yolk
- mayonnaise
- a thickener like corn starch, xanthan, or guar gum

FLAVORING/SEASONING:
Anything that will enhance the flavor of the dressing
- sea salt and pepper
- herbs and spices
- soy sauce, fish sauce, tamari, coconut aminos
- hot sauce, chili paste, umami paste
- juice (orange juice or pomegranate, for example)
- sweetener (sugar or sugar substitute)
- shallots, garlic, ginger, sesame seeds, poppy seeds
- anchovies

THE FORMULA:
I prefer a lower-fat vinaigrette so I use more vinegar than olive oil. I always use a mason jar to mix the ingredients to keep it super simple and to store the remaining dressing.

- 1/4 cup vinegar/acid
- 1–2 tbsp oil/fat
- 1 tsp emulsifier
- any additional seasonings to enhance the flavor

A VINAIGRETTE DRESSING TAKES JUST SECONDS TO MAKE.
Master this concept and you'll be able to whip up a delicious salad anytime.

Just a few simple components make up every dressing.
Mix and match to create your own favorites.

I always keep mason jars in different sizes so I can shake up a dressing or sauce and store it for later all in one container.

TO SUPREME (SEGMENT)
a grapefruit or an orange, first cut off the top and bottom of the fruit to give you a flat surface. Slice off all the skin and white pith. Then cut out segments of fruit between the membranes, leaving you with a nice tender piece of fruit.

GRAPEFRUIT SALAD

246 calories, 30.8 g protein, 15.7 g carbs, 6.8 g fat, 4g fiber

4 servings—4 oz. of chicken per serving

INGREDIENTS:

- 1 lb boneless skinless chicken breast, butterflied
- 8 cups spring mix salad greens
- 1 small grapefruit (196 g), supreme (save the leftover membrane for the juice)
- 112 g or 4 oz. fat-free feta
- handful fresh mint, chopped
- 1tsp per serving (4 servings) olive oil
- 2 tbsp per serving (4 servings) sherry vinegar
- sea salt and freshly ground pepper

DIRECTIONS:

Start with the butterflied chicken breasts. Thin-sliced breasts cook faster and all the way though much better than a thicker cut. Over medium high heat, heat a large skillet and coat with cooking spray.

Season chicken with salt and pepper and cook on one side for 4–6 minutes until you have a nice golden color. Flip the chicken over and use the juice from the grapefruit membrane to add flavor to the chicken as it continues to cook. Once the chicken reaches an internal temperature of 165 degrees remove from heat, tent with foil, and allow to rest while you prepare the rest of the salad.

Arrange the salad with the remaining ingredients. For the most accurate nutrition facts arrange each plate individually. Each serving of salad gets 1 tsp of olive oil and 2 tbsp of vinegar, plus salt and pepper.

Once the chicken has rested add it to the top of the salad and serve.

GRILLED ROMAINE SALAD

307 calories, 12 g protein, 27 g carbs, 17 g fat, 7 g fiber   Serves 4

Calculated without added chicken

INGREDIENTS:

- 2 whole heads romaine lettuce cut in half lengthwise
- 4 tbsp goat cheese or fat-free feta
- 1/4 cup chopped walnuts
- pinch of cayenne pepper (optional)
- 2 tbsp Splenda brown sugar
- 1/4 cup dried cranberries
- balsamic vinaigrette or balsamic reduction and olive oil
- sea salt and pepper

DIRECTIONS:

Heat a small skillet, spray with a tiny bit of cooking spray, put in the chopped walnuts and sugar, and cook until the sugar melts, stirring frequently. It can burn quick, so don't take your eyes off of it.

Remove from heat and allow to cool.

Grill the romaine over medium low heat just to char the edges, flat side down. Remove.

To dress sprinkle walnuts, goat cheese, and cranberries (1 tbsp per half head of lettuce), then drizzle with 1 tbsp balsamic vinegar and 1 tsp olive oil per serving.

SEARED AHI TUNA SALAD

252 calories, 30.5 g protein, 11.2 g carbs, 8.5 g fat, 2 g fiber   Serves 4

INGREDIENTS:

- 1 lb sashimi-grade ahi filets
- about 1/4 cup Japanese furikake to coat tuna filets
- 8 cups arugula
- 1 tsp per serving olive oil
- 2 tbsp balsamic vinegar per serving
- 2–3 tbsp ahi poke marinade (see recipe on page 39)

DIRECTIONS:

Coat the tuna filets in furikake. Sear over medium high heat on all sides about 30 seconds to a minute per side.

Slice ahi filets and place over dressed salad. Spoon over the top some of the ahi marinade mixture.

YOU CAN FIND JAPANESE FURIKAKE SEASONING in the spice aisle or the international food section of the grocery store. It is a dry blend of sesame seeds, seaweed, mirin, and soy sauce. If you can't find it, sesame seeds will work.

THIS IS A GREAT RECIPE FOR LEFTOVER CHICKEN or a rotisserie chicken from the grocery store in a pinch.

I will also make a big batch of this for a big group. It's super healthy and the cabbage stands up to soaking in the dressing just like a slaw. I will load up on this instead of other unhealthy party foods.

MEXICAN CABBAGE SALAD

213 calories, 23.4 g protein, 13.7 g carbs, 6.6 g fat, 4.3 g fiber   Serves 4

INGREDIENTS:

- 1 lb boneless skinless chicken breasts
- 1 cup water
- 1 tbsp soy sauce, tamari, or coconut aminos
- 8 cups shredded cabbage or preshredded coleslaw package
- 1/2 finely sliced red onion
- about 3 finely sliced radishes
- 1 finely sliced serrano pepper, to taste
- 1 finely sliced jalapeño pepper, to taste
- 2 tbsp chopped cilantro
- 1–2 limes (for juicing)
- 1 tbsp mild flavored oil (macadamia nut, canola, olive)
- 1/4 cup apple cider vinegar
- sea salt and freshly ground pepper

DIRECTIONS:

I use a slow cooker to poach my chicken, but you can also use a pot of boiling water. I add soy sauce or coconut amino to flavor the chicken as it poaches. Cook the chicken until it shreds easily with a fork. Mix the cabbage, red onion, radish, peppers (depending on how much spice you like), and shredded chicken. Season with salt and pepper, and dress with the juice of a lime and olive oil. Toss to combine, and eat right away, or make ahead and leave in the fridge until ready to serve.

SHRIMP CEVICHE SALAD

249 calories, 26 g protein, 21 g carbs, 7 g fat, 6.2 g fiber   Serves 4

INGREDIENTS:

- 1 lb raw peeled deveined shrimp
- 1 cup orange juice and 2 cups water
- 1 tsp sea salt
- 1 bay leaf
- 1 lemon, 1/2 orange, 2 limes; save the fruit for the recipe
- 2 tbsp cilantro, chopped
- 180 g jicama, diced
- 200 g or 1 medium zucchini, diced
- 230 g or 1 large tomato, diced
- 115 g or 1 med white onion, diced
- 115 g or 1 small avocado, diced
- 14 g or 1 jalapeño pepper, diced
- 2 tbsp amaranth seeds
- salt and pepper

DIRECTIONS:

First squeeze the juice from the orange, lemon, and limes. Set aside. Next, in a pot pour the 1 cup orange juice, water, salt, bay leaf, and the squeezed fruits. Bring to a boil over medium high heat; allow the flavor to infuse for a few minutes. Reduce to medium low heat and add the shrimp. Simmer uncovered for 5 minutes until the shrimp turns bright pink. Chill and chop into bite sized pieces before adding to the rest of the ingredients.

Combine the remaining ingredients and toss until well mixed. Once the shrimp is chilled, add it to the mixture.

THIS CEVICHE SALAD is hearty and chunkier than a traditional recipe. Great to eat alone, without chips or bread, making it much lighter.

YOU CAN MAKE THIS FAMILY STYLE and serve it as a large salad on one plate, or you can make individual servings.

1 SERVING = 1 chicken breast, 2 cups arugula, 3 tomatoes, 1 tsp olive oil, and 2 tbsp balsamic vinegar.

LEMON CHICKEN AND ARUGULA
194 calories, 27.61 g protein, 5.23 g carbs, 8.85 g fat, 3.5 g fiber   4 servings

INGREDIENTS:

- 1 lb boneless skinless chicken breasts, butterflied
- the juice of 1 lemon, plus another lemon sliced
- 1 tsp minced garlic
- 1 tsp dried oregano
- about 12 grape tomatoes
- sea salt and freshly ground pepper
- 8 cups arugula
- 1 tbsp + 1 tsp olive oil
- 1/4 cup balsamic vinegar
- 4–5 fresh basil leaves, chiffonade (roll up like a cigar and slice into thin strips)

DIRECTIONS:

Preheat oven to 350 degrees F. 1 pound of chicken breasts should yield 4 thin sliced breasts. In a glass baking dish place 4 chicken breast filets. Over the chicken, add the zest of the lemon and the juice. Sprinkle with the oregano, garlic, and salt and pepper. Add the tomatoes and sliced lemon on top. Bake in the oven 30–45 minutes until chicken reaches 165 degrees F. Tent the chicken and allow to rest for 10–15 minutes. Serve over a bed of arugula dressed with olive oil, vinegar, salt, and pepper and top with a few fresh bass leaves

GREEK CHICKEN SALAD

254 calories, 31.75 g protein, 21 g carbs, 7 g fat, 6 g fiber   Serves 4

MARINADE INGREDIENTS:

- 1 lb boneless skinless chicken breasts, butterflied
- 1/4 cup red wine vinegar
- 1 tsp yellow mustard
- 1 tsp black pepper
- 2 tsp dried oregano
- 2 tsp garlic powder
- the juice from 1 lemon
- 1 small or 1/2 of a large shallot, minced

SALAD INGREDIENTS:

- 8 cups romaine lettuce
- 1 tbsp + 1 tsp olive oil
- 1/4 cup red wine vinegar
- 200 g cucumber, sliced
- 200 g tomato, quartered or small cherry tomatoes
- 60 g onion, sliced
- 112 g or 4 oz. low-fat or fat-free feta

DIRECTIONS:

Butterfly the chicken breasts so there is more surface area for the marinade and a faster cooking time. Mix all the ingredients for the marinade and place into a large zip-top bag. Let sit in the refrigerator for 30 minutes to an hour. Cook on an indoor or outdoor grill until the chicken reaches an internal temperature of 165 degrees F. Allow the chicken to rest for 10–15 minutes before slicing. Arrange the salad by topping with the remaining ingredients.

SALADS ARE A GREAT LOW CARB MEAL, but if you have the luxury of more carbs in your diet or this is a post-workout meal, add some pita bread and some low-fat tzatziki.

Other tasty topping options for a Greek salad are banana peppers, olives, and pickled beets.

ENTREES

Tilapia fish tacos

Garlic and rosemary pork tenderloin

Coffee-crusted pork

Low-carb lasagna

Spiced maple chicken

Spicy Korean chicken with kimchi slaw

Rosemary turkey loaf

Mexican frittata

Pizza frittata

Cauliflower pizza crust

Vanilla-glazed orange roughy

Orange chicken

Homemade Mexican turkey

Zucchini carbonara

TILAPIA FISH TACOS

450 calories, 35.81 g protein, 37 g carbs, 20 g fat, 7.5 g fiber   4 servings

INGREDIENTS:

- 1 tbsp extra virgin olive oil
- 2 garlic cloves, minced
- 1 jalapeño, minced
- 1 tsp paprika
- ground pepper
- 1 lb tilapia filets
- 2 cups shredded cabbage
- 1 single-serving container plain fat-free Greek yogurt, divided
- 2 tbsp mayonnaise
- 1 large avocado, about 200 g
- 2 tsp garlic, divided
- 2 tbsp lime juice
- 8 small corn tortillas
- cilantro and limes for serving

DIRECTIONS:

In a gallon plastic bag combine olive oil, garlic, chiles, paprika, and pepper. Place tilapia in the bag and coat with mixture. Refrigerate for 30 minutes to 4 hours.

In a small bowl mix 2 tbsp of the yogurt, 1 tsp garlic, and mayo. Set aside for serving.

In a food processor combine half yogurt, avocado, lime juice, and 1 tsp garlic; season with salt and pepper.

In a large skillet cook the tilapia fillets for about 3 min per side. They are done when they start to flake. Flake them slightly so they are bite sized.

To create the tacos on each tortilla, spread about a tbsp of the avocado puree as the base, place the fish and some cabbage and cilantro. Top with the white sauce. Garnish with a lime wedge.

GARLIC AND ROSEMARY PORK TENDERLOIN

136 calories, 23.8 g protein, 0 g carbs, 3.8 g fat, 0 g fiber   per 4 oz. portion

INGREDIENTS:

- 1 lb pork tenderloin (fat trimmed)
- sea salt and pepper
- a few sprigs of fresh rosemary
- 6–8 garlic cloves

DIRECTIONS:

Preheat oven to 350 degrees F. Season the pork with salt and pepper. With a paring knife, cut six to eight slits along the pork to about the middle of the tenderloin. In each slit stuff a whole garlic clove. Cut the rosemary into 2-inch sprigs. Poke smaller slits to put the rosemary sprigs into the pork in the same manner. Roast the pork in the oven until the internal temperature reads 150 degrees F. Cover with aluminum foil and allow to rest 15 minutes before slicing.

SUPER SIMPLE
but an impressive presentation!

THIS IS ALSO
a great rub for beef!

COFFEE-CRUSTED PORK
136 calories, 23.8 g protein, 0 g carbs, 3.8 g fat, 0 g fiber   per 4 oz. portion

INGREDIENTS:

- 2 tbsp ground coffee (toffee or caramel flavor)
- 1/4 tsp black pepper
- 1/2 tsp sea salt
- 2 stevia packets
- 1/8 tsp cayenne pepper
- 1 lb pork tenderloin

DIRECTIONS:

Pre-heat the oven to 350. In a gallon sized zip top bag mix together coffee, salt, pepper, stevia, and cayenne pepper. Once combined add the pork and coat with the mixture. Roast the pork in the oven until the internal temperature reads 150 degrees F. cover with aluminum foil and allow to rest 15 minutes before slicing.

LOW-CARB LASAGNA

160 calories, 20.9 g protein, 11 g carbs, 3.8 g fat, 2.9 g fiber   9 servings

INGREDIENTS:

- 3 medium zucchini
- 1 lb extra lean ground beef or ground turkey
- 1 jar marinara sauce, low fat
- 1 lb fat free cottage cheese
- 80 g or 3 oz. part skim mozzarella
- 1 14 oz. can artichokes, quartered

DIRECTIONS:

Preheat the oven to 350 degrees F. Brown the ground beef in a large skillet. Drain off any excess fat. Add the marinara sauce and allow to simmer over low heat to let the flavor to infuse into the meat.

While the meat is cooking, slice the zucchini lengthwise into long strips about 1/8 in. thick. Get your other ingredients ready to arrange.

In a 9 x 13 baking dish start out with a thin layer of the sauce first. In a single layer arrange the zucchini noodles. Next spoon a thin layer of the meat sauce along the noodles, about a tbsp of cottage cheese every 2 inches; alternate with an artichoke heart. Sprinkle with a little of the shredded cheese. Add another layer of noodles and repeat until you have three layers the top layer exposed (no zucchini).

Bake for 30 minutes, until the cheese is melted and the sauce is bubbly.

USE YOUR FAVORITE JARRED MARINARA sauce for a quick weeknight dinner you can prepare in advance. Look for one that has no added sugar and is low in fat.

SPICY MAPLE CHICKEN

122 calories, 2.55 g fat, .5 g carbs, 22.6 g protein   4 servings

INGREDIENTS:

- 2 (8 oz.) chicken breasts, boneless, skinless, butterflied
- 2 tbsp Greek yogurt, fat free
- 2 tbsp Walden Farms maple syrup
- 2 tsp smoked paprika
- 1 tsp cayenne pepper or to taste
- salt and pepper to taste

DIRECTIONS:

Combine all ingredients in a zip top bag and marinate for 1 hour max. The yogurt will tenderize the chicken but don't let it sit too long. Grill and serve.

Garnish the finished dish with chive pesto and Sriracha.

CHIVE PESTO

1 tsp serving =
35 calories, 4 g fat

INGREDIENTS:

- 4 tbsp olive oil
- 1 bunch chives, about 18 g

DIRECTIONS:

Combine in a food processor or blender until smooth.

ROSEMARY TURKEY LOAF

235 calories, 28.3 g protein, 22 g carbs, 3.2 g fat, 3 g fiber   4 servings

INGREDIENTS:

- 1 1/4 lb extra lean ground turkey (20 oz.)
- 2 shitake mushrooms, dried (5 g)
- 1/2 tsp fish sauce
- 1/4 cup dry old fashioned oats
- 1 tbsp fresh or 1/2 tbsp dry rosemary
- 1 extra large egg
- 1/4 cup balsamic vinegar
- sea salt and pepper

TOPPING:

- 1/3 cup reduced sugar ketchup
- 2 tbsp brown sugar or sweetener of choice
- 1 tbsp yellow mustard

DIRECTIONS:

Preheat oven to 350 degrees. In a mini food processor or blender combine the mushrooms and fish sauce with about 1/4 cup of the ground turkey. Puree until you get a smooth paste.

In a medium-sized bowl combine the paste with the rest of the ingredients and mix gently until combined. You don't want to overwork it.

Place mixture in a loaf pan or on a lined baking sheet that has been sprayed with cooking spray, and shape into an even loaf shape.

Mix the topping ingredients together and spread over the loaf.

Bake for 45 minutes, until cooked through.

THIS DISH IS SWEET, SAVORY, AND HOT,
and the kimchi adds an acidic bite that balances it all out.
If you're not a fan of kimchi leave it out—it's delicious without it as well.

Kimchi is a fermented cabbage side dish. It is spicy and acidic in taste.
It takes a long time to make it yourself, so the jarred version is great.
It is found in the refrigerated asian food section, usually where you can
also find wonton wrappers and tofu. It is a great low-calorie condiment
common in Korean cooking.

SPICY KOREAN CHICKEN WITH KIMCHI SLAW

231 calories, 30 g protein, 21.6 g carbs, 2.8 g fat, 6 g fiber

1 serving = 4 oz. chicken (113g) 2 cups (200g) cabbage slaw,100 g kimchi, 50 g (3 tbsp) dressing

DRY RUB INGREDIENTS:

- 1 lb boneless skinless chicken breast, butterflied for quicker cook time
- 1 tsp onion powder
- 1 tsp garlic powder
- 2 tbsp Korean chili flakes (gochugaru)
- 1 tsp salt
- 1/4 tsp pepper

SLAW DRESSING INGREDIENTS:

- 8 cups cabbage or slaw mix, shredded
- 1/2 cup coconut aminos
- 2 tbsp rice vinegar
- 1 tsp sesame oil
- 1 tbsp swerve or preferred sweetener
- 1/2 tbsp Korean chili flakes (gochugaru)
- 1 tsp minced ginger
- 1 tsp minced garlic

Toss with shredded cabbage and garnish with jarred kimchi (chopped into bite-sized pieces)

DIRECTIONS:

Combine all of the ingredients for the dry rub. Coat the chicken. Heat a skillet over medium high heat. Coat the pan with nonstick spray. Cook the chicken about 6 minutes per side, depending on the thickness of the breasts. Once the chicken reaches an internal temperature of 165 degrees F remove from heat, tent it with foil, and allow to rest for 10–15 minutes.

To prepare the dressing, I always use a jar to shake up, seal, and store the leftovers. Combine all ingredients for the dressing. To plate, toss the dressing with the cabbage, top with some jarred kimchi, and add cooked chicken.

MEXICAN FRITTATA

240 calories, 39.7 g protein, 13.6 g carb, 1.8 g fat, 3 g fiber per serving

INGREDIENTS:

- 200 g or 7 oz. egg whites
- 1 tbsp fat-free cream cheese
- 1 tbsp nutritional yeast
- sea salt

TOPPINGS:

- 50 g or 2 oz. green bell pepper, sliced
- 30 g or 1 oz. onion, sliced
- 20 g or 1 oz. fat-free cheese, shredded
- 50 g or 2 oz. enchilada sauce, canned

DIRECTIONS:

First, preheat the oven to 350 degrees F. Heat a small oven-safe skillet over medium heat. Beat the eggs, cream cheese, and nutritional yeast. Spray the pan with nonstick spray and once heated add the egg mixture. Once the bottom has cooked for 2–3 minutes add the toppings and place in the oven. It's done when the eggs are set and the cheese is melted, about 3–5 minutes.

I MAKE INDIVIDUAL-SIZED frittatas so you can customize the ingredients.

Great for breakfast, lunch, or dinner.

PIZZA FRITTATA

268 calories, 41.2 g protein, 16 g carbs, 2.1 g fat, 5 g fiber per serving

INGREDIENTS:

- 200 g or 7 oz. egg whites
- 1 tbsp fat free cream cheese
- 1 tbsp nutritional yeast
- sea salt

TOPPINGS:

- 50 g or 2 oz. artichoke, sliced
- 40 g or 2 oz. fat-free cheese, shredded
- 50 g or 2 oz. tomato sauce or pizza sauce, canned (look for one that's low in fat)

DIRECTIONS:

First, preheat the oven to 350 degrees F. Heat a small oven-safe skillet over medium heat. Beat the eggs, cream cheese, and nutritional yeast. Spray the pan with nonstick spray and once heated add the egg mixture. Once the bottom has cooked for 2–3 minutes add the toppings and place in the oven. It's done when the eggs are set and the cheese is melted, about 3–5 minutes.

CAULIFLOWER CRUST

209 calories, 24 g protein, 32 g carbs, <1 g fat, 15 g fiber   2 servings

INGREDIENTS:

- 2 medium heads cauliflower, about 575 g each
- 2 egg whites, beaten
- 1 tbsp fat-free cream cheese
- 1 oz. shredded fat-free cheese
- 1 tbsp nutritional yeast
- 1 tsp dried oregano
- 1/2 tsp sea salt and cracked pepper

DIRECTIONS:

Preheat the oven to 400 degrees F. Grate the raw cauliflower in a food processor or on a hand grater. Steam the cauliflower until tender. You can do this in the microwave in a large glass bowl covered with plastic wrap. Once it's cool enough to handle, place the steamed cauliflower in a dish towel and ring out all the excess water. (It's a lot of water!) In a medium bowl, add the rest of the ingredients and mix well. Coat a baking sheet with tin foil and a quick spray of cooking spray. Divide the dough in half and shape into two rectangles about 1/4 in. thick. You can make the edges a little thicker to mimic the crust. Bake for about 20 minutes, until it's golden and is solid enough to move. Transfer to a wire rack, by flipping it over and carefully pulling the foil off. Place the rack back on the baking sheet and continue to cook for about 10 more minutes. The wire rack allows air to get all around the crust and to get it nice and crispy.

USE YOUR FAVORITE JARRED MARINARA sauce for a quick weeknight dinner you can prepare in advance. Look for one that has no added sugar and is low in fat.

SUPER SIMPLE AND FAST!

Try the vanilla glaze on
steamed cauliflower.

VANILLA GLAZED ORANGE ROUGHY

99 calories, 20 g protein,1.5 g carbs, <1 g fat, 0 g fiber   per 4 oz. serving

INGREDIENTS:

- orange roughy fillets
- cooking spray
- 1 tsp swerve, confectioner's style (powdered)
- 1/2 tsp vanilla bean paste
- 1tbsp water
- pinch sea salt (I use truffle salt for this)

DIRECTIONS:

Heat a nonstick skillet over high heat. You want to get a good sear on the fish, so make sure it's really hot before you put it on. Just a small spray of cooking spray will keep it from sticking. Sear both sides until golden brown. While the fish is cooking mix the swerve, vanilla, and water. Just before serving pour the vanilla mixture over the fish and sprinkle with sea salt.

ORANGE CHICKEN

170 calories, 26 g protein, 14 g carbs, 1.4 g fat, 3.5 g fiber   makes 4 - 4oz servings

INGREDIENTS:

- 1 pound boneless skinless chicken breasts, cubed
- 3 tbsp corn starch
- 1/2 cup or 120 g sugar free orange marmalade
- 1 tbsp rice vinegar
- 1 tbsp coconut aminos or soy sauce
- 1/2 tsp ginger, minced
- 1/2 tsp garlic, minced
- 1/2 to 1 tsp chili flakes, to taste
- 1 scallion, sliced for garnish

DIRECTIONS:

Heat a skillet over medium high heat. Toss chicken with corn starch until well coated. Cook chicken in the pan with a a light spray of cooking spray. While the chicken is cooking combine the remaining ingredients except for the scallion for the sauce. When the chicken pieces are cooked through and golden brown, add the sauce over low heat and toss to combine. Garnish with fresh sliced scallion. Great served with brown rice, or shiritake noodles for a lower carb option.

A HEALTHIER VERSION
of Chinese take-out at home.

HOMEMADE MEXICAN TURKEY

34.5 calories, 1.6 g protein, 6.4 g carbs, .9 g fat, 2.2 g fiber for the seasoning alone   4 servings
154 calories, 27.6 g protein, 6.4 g carbs, 2.4 g fat, 2.2 g fiber per 4 oz. portion with ground turkey

INGREDIENTS:

- 1 1/4 pound extra lean ground turkey (20 oz.)
- 2 tbsp chili powder
- 1 tbsp garlic powder
- 1 tbsp onion powder
- 1 tbsp cumin
- 1 tbsp apple cider vinegar
- 1 tbsp tomato paste
- 1 1/4 cup water
- sea salt and pepper

DIRECTIONS:

In a skillet over medium high heat brown your meat of choice. Once cooked turn the heat to low, and add the remaining ingredients. Mix well and allow to reduce for about 10 minutes until the sauce begins to thicken.

NO NEED TO GO TO THE STORE for a seasoning packet. Make it at home with what's in your pantry.

Way less sodium and sugar than store bought. I like to use 99% lean ground turkey, but you can sub any protein like chicken, pork or beef.

Make your own baked tortilla chips with store bought low carb tortillas. Just slice, lightly coat with cooking spray and bake until crispy.

ZUCCHINI CARBONARA

205 calories, 26.5 g protein, 10 g carbs, 6.5 g fat, 3 g fiber   1 serving

INGREDIENTS:

- 1 medium zucchini, spirilized
- 1 egg
- 2 oz. smoked ham, cubed (low fat)
- 1 oz. fat free feta cheese
- black pepper to taste
- sea salt (with truffle, optional)

DIRECTIONS:

Spirilize the zucchini, and chop the ham into cubes. Heat the zucchini and ham over medium heat in a medium skillet, just to warm through. Beat the egg in a seperate bowl and add the feta. After a few minutes, when the zucchini is slightly tender remove from the heat and stir in the egg mixture in the same pan. Season with truffle sea salt and pepper.

*You can add some frozen peas to the ham and zucchini or garnish with some fresh chopped parsley.

THIS IS ONE OF MY FAVORITE pasta dishes, but it's typically loaded with fat and carbs.

Try this super quick guilt free version instead.

You can also use turkey bacon, but the fat content may be slightly higher.

SIDE DISHES

Chile relleno

Savory or sweet squash wedges

Cauliflower risotto

Cauliflower mash

Cauliflower tabbouleh

Squash slaw

Asian stir-fry broccoli

Eggplant spears

Quick pickled cucumber salad

Chile lime cucumbers

Roasted radishes

Roasted Brussels sprouts with turkey bacon

Roasted sun chokes with turkey bacon

Mango salsa

Sautéed mushrooms and leeks

Coconut rice

Asian carrot and jicama slaw

Creamy zucchini

CHILE RELLENO

136 calories, 19.6 g protein, 10.5 g carbs,1 g fat, 1.7 g fiber   4 servings

INGREDIENTS:

- 4 pasilla peppers, or green bell peppers if you don't like heat
- 1 cup low-fat or fat-free cottage cheese
- 40 g or 1 oz. fat-free or low-fat shredded cheese
- 1/4 cup or 63 g enchilada sauce with no fat
- 1/2 to 1 tsp red pepper flakes
- sea salt and freshly ground pepper
- green onion, to garnish

DIRECTIONS:

Preheat the oven to 350 degrees F. Carefully with tongs roast the chills directly over a gas burner. Just set them right on the grates and turn them until they char and turn black. Place the hot peppers into a zip top bag and let them steam for 5–10 minutes. With a towel carefully wipe off the black parts from the peppers; do not rinse. Try not to rip the peppers open. Cut a slit in each pepper lengthwise and remove the seeds and some of the membrane. Fill each pepper with two heaping tablespoons full of cottage cheese, and place in a baking dish. Top with enchilada sauce, red pepper flakes, sea salt, pepper, and shredded cheese. Bake for about 25 minutes, until cheese is melted and the sauce is bubbly. Garnish with sliced green onion.

EXCELLENT AS A LOW-CARB SIDE DISH

or as an entree. The cottage cheese is a great source of protein.

I use a store-bought enchilada sauce. There are plenty of varieties that are low in fat and carbs. No need to make it yourself. Quick and easy for a weeknight meal.

A GREAT LOW-CARB and low-cal alternative to fries. Make the sweet version as a low-cal dessert. Quick and easy for a weeknight meal. You can save the seeds and roast them too!

SAVORY OR SWEET SQUASH WEDGES

74 calories, 2.5 g protein, 22.2 g carbs, 0 g fat, 2.5 g fiber   per 200 g serving

SAVORY INGREDIENTS:

- 1 kabocha squash or 2 smaller delicata squashes
- garlic powder
- onion powder
- paprika
- chili powder
- sea salt
- cooking spray

SWEET INGREDIENTS:

- 1 kabocha squash or 2 smaller delicata squashes
- Granulated stevia or swerve
- pumpkin pie spice
- sea salt
- cooking spray (I use coconut oil pray on the sweet version, but any will work)

DIRECTIONS:

Preheat the oven to 400 degrees F. Line two sheet trays with aluminum foil or parchment. Wash the squash well before slicing, since you can eat the skin with these varieties. Slice into wedges that are about the same thickness. I usually make one tray of savory and one tray of sweet. Coat the trays lightly with cooking spray, and arrange the wedges in a single layer. Give them another quick spray and sprinkle the ingredients over top. Place in the oven and roast for about 20 minutes. Halfway through take them out, flip them over, and season the other side. Keep an eye on them so they don't burn; if they are thinner they will cook quickly.

CAULIFLOWER RISOTTO

87 calories, 6 g protein, 10 g carbs, 4 g fat, 5 g fiber

4 servings

INGREDIENTS:

- 1 medium head cauliflower, grated (575 g)
- 1 cup or 86 g oyster mushrooms, chopped
- 2 tbsp nutritional yeast
- 1/3 cup chicken broth
- salt and pepper to taste
- 1 tbsp olive oil infused with black or white truffles

DIRECTIONS:

In a large sauté pan over medium high heat add all of the ingredients except for the oil and allow the cauliflower to soften and the mushrooms to cook. When cooked drizzle the truffle oil over the top, mix and serve.

CAULIFLOWER IS SO VERSATILE.

It can be a wonderful substitute for higher-carb dishes in so many recipes.

Mushrooms add a meaty flavor to the risotto. My favorites are oyster mushrooms, but any will work.

A GREAT ALTERNATIVE
to potatoes!

CAULIFLOWER MASH

168 calories, 8.4 g protein, 22.4 g carbs, 7.5 g fat, 10.6 g fiber per serving

2 large servings

INGREDIENTS:

- 1 head cauliflower
- 1 tbsp butter flavored olive oil
- 1/2 tsp truffle sea salt
- 1/4 cup unsweetened almond milk

DIRECTIONS:

Steam the cauliflower until tender. I used a pressure cooker and cooked it for 6 minutes, but a steamer or a microwave will work for this as well. Add the remaining ingredients and blend until smooth.

CAULIFLOWER TABBOULEH

169 calories, 4 g protein, 26 g carbs, 7 g fat, 5 g fiber per serving   4 servings

INGREDIENTS:

- 1 medium head cauliflower, about 575 g
- 1 cup cherry tomatoes, halved
- 1/2 cup golden raisins (you can also use dates, pomegranate arils, currants, or dried cranberries)
- 1 bunch parsley and/or mint chopped (about 1/2 cup)
- 2 tbsp red wine vinegar
- 2 tbsp olive oil
- salt and pepper to taste

DIRECTIONS:

Grate the raw cauliflower using a food processor or box grater. Combine the remaining ingredients and allow to chill and absorb the flavors before serving.

BUTTERNUT SQUASH SLAW

114 calories, 3.5 g protein, 20 g carbs, 3 g fat, 4 g fiber

8 servings, about 200 g per serving

INGREDIENTS:

- about 1,000 g whole butternut squash (around 850 g after peeling and seeding)
- 2 granny smith apples (about 400 g total), shredded
- 1/4 cup (35 g) walnuts, chopped
- 1 med zucchini, shredded (200 g)
- 2 green onions/chives, chopped
- 1/4 cup parsley, chopped
- sea salt and pepper

DRESSING INGREDIENTS:

- 3 oz. fat-free cream cheese
- 1/2 cup apple cider vinegar
- 1/4 cup sugar-free maple syrup
- sea salt and pepper

DIRECTIONS:

Shred the raw squash, apple, and zucchini in a food processor. Add the walnuts, green onion/chives, and parsley. Mix. In a jar or small bowl mix together the dressing ingredients. Once combined and creamy toss with the slaw. Allow to chill and absorb the flavors before serving.

ASIAN STIR-FRY BROCCOLI

79 calories, 3.3 g protein, 14 g carbs, 1 g fat, 2 g fiber

per 1 cup of broccoli and 2 tbsp of prepared sauce

INGREDIENTS:

- 1 head Broccoli, cut into florets

STIR-FRY SAUCE INGREDIENTS:

- 2–3 green onions, diced whites and greens
- 1/2 teaspoon freshly grated fresh ginger
  (I keep fresh ginger peeled and in the freezer,
  so I always have it on hand)
- 3 finely diced garlic cloves
- 1/2 cup coconut aminos
- 1 tsp sesame oil
- 1/2 tsp red pepper flakes
- 1 tsp Sriracha
- 1 tsp sea salt

DIRECTIONS:

Cut broccoli into florets. Lightly steam or blanch the broccoli to soften.

Combine all other ingredients in a jar or small sealable container. Heat a skillet over medium high heat. Lightly coat with cooking spray; add the broccoli and 2 tbsp of sauce per 1 cup of broccoli. Toss to coat and heat thoroughly.

EGGPLANT SPEARS

68 calories, .5 g fat, 16 g carbs, 2.5 g protein, 8 g fiber   2 servings

INGREDIENTS:

- 1 eggplant, about 548 g, or 1.25 lbs.
- salt and pepper to taste

DIRECTIONS:

Slice the eggplant into strips. Lay out on paper towels and sprinkle with sea salt. Allow the eggplant to sweat for about 30 minutes. This will remove the bitterness. Give it a quick rinse and dry well. Preheat the oven to 425–450 degrees F. I use convection for this recipe to get it crispier. As a general rule for convection cooking you can reduce the temperature by 25 degrees F. 425 degrees for convection, or regular bake at 450 degrees. On a baking sheet lined with foil and a quick spray of cooking spray arrange the spears in a single layer. It may take two baking sheets. Spray the top of the spears so the salt and pepper will stick and bake for about 20 minutes, until golden brown and crispy.

EXPERIMENT WITH YOUR FAVORITE SPICES and creating new flavorful pickles. Homemade pickles are usually much lower in sodium.

This is a great low-calorie snack!

QUICK PICKLED CUCUMBER SALAD

26 calories, 1 g protein, 6 g carbs, 0 g fat, 1 g fiber   2 servings

INGREDIENTS:

- 1 cucumber, about 300 g
- 1 tsp red chili flakes
- 1 1/2 tbsp white vinegar, apple cider vinegar, or rice vinegar
- 1 tsp dill
- salt and pepper to taste

DIRECTIONS:

Slice the cucumber, and add the remaining ingredients. This can be eaten right away, unlike a traditional pickle.

CHILE LIME CUCUMBERS

29 calories, 1 g protein, 7.5 g carbs, 0 g fat, .75 g fiber   2 servings

INGREDIENTS:

- 1 cucumber, about 300 g
- 1 tsp Korean chili flakes (gochugaru)
- juice of 1 lime
- salt and pepper to taste

DIRECTIONS:

Slice the cucumber, and add the remaining ingredients.

GOCHUGARU
is a Korean red chili powder that has a sweet flavor and some heat. If you can't find it in the international food section of the grocery store, it is easy to find online. You can substitute another type of chili as well.

ALMOST TOO GOOD TO BE TRUE!
So low in calories, yet so delicious!

You can even save the greens for a salad.

Roasted radishes have a potato-like texture and taste! They are much milder in flavor when roasted.

ROASTED RADISHES
7 calories, .3 g protein, 1.5 g carbs, 0 g fat, .7 g fiber   2 servings

INGREDIENTS:

- 2 bunches of radishes, about 10
- sea salt and pepper

DIRECTIONS:

Preheat the oven to 400 degrees F. Wash and remove the stems of the radishes. Sometimes I slice them, and sometimes I leave them whole. Just make sure they are all relatively the same size so they cook at the same rate. On a foil-lined baking sheet coated with a light cooking spray. Arrange the radishes in a single layer. Season with salt and pepper and roast for 15–20 minutes until tender.

BRUSSELS SPROUTS WITH TURKEY BACON

98 calories, 6 g protein, 13 g carbs, 3.8 g fat, 4.5 g fiber   4 servings

INGREDIENTS:

- 1 lb Brussels sprouts
- 3 strips turkey bacon, cut into lardons (strips)
- 1 shallot (sliced)
- 1/2 tbsp olive oil
- sherry vinegar
- salt and pepper to taste

DIRECTIONS:

Wash and trim the brown ends off the Brussels sprouts. Cut in half or quarter so they are all the same size. Steam just until tender and set aside.

In a large sauté pan over medium high heat with a bit of cooking spray cook the bacon and shallots. Remove from the pan, and set aside. In the same pan with olive oil put in the sprouts, arrange in a single layer, and allow them to sit so they caramelize in the bacon and shallot flavor. Remember to season with salt and pepper. After a few minutes, or when you start to see the Brussels sprouts brown, flip them over to brown the other side. At the very end of cooking toss in the bacon and shallots, stir and drizzle with sherry vinegar

ROASTED SUNCHOKES

109 calories, 4 g protein, 20 g carbs, 1.7 g fat, 2 g fiber   4 servings

INGREDIENTS:

- sunchokes or Jerusalem artichokes
- 3 slices turkey bacon
- cooking spray
- Cajun spice blend
- salt and pepper

DIRECTIONS:

Heat the oven to 400 degrees F. Wash and chop sunchokes into bite sized pieces. Slice turkey bacon into lardons and season with cajun spice blend. This is easily found in the spice aisle of the grocery store. On a baking sheet lined with foil and a light coating of cooking spray add the sunchokes and bacon and sprinkle with salt and pepper to taste. Roast for about 20 minutes until softened and browned on the edges.

HAS THE FLAVOR
of an artichoke, more like a low-carb potato. You can roast, boil, and mash or eat them raw.

GREAT ON ITS OWN,
as a topping, or a dip.

MANGO SALSA
51 calories, 8 g protein, 12 g carbs, .23 g fat, 4 g fiber   4 servings

INGREDIENTS:

- 1 ripe mango, seeded and diced
- 1 jalapeño pepper, seeded, and diced
- 1/2 onion, diced
- 1 cup cherry tomatoes, quartered
- 1 handful cilantro, chopped
- sea salt and pepper

DIRECTIONS:

Mix all ingredients. Allow to sit in the fridge for 30 minutes for flavors to meld.

SAUTÉED MUSHROOMS AND LEEKS

41 calories, 2 g protein, 9 g carbs, 0 g fat, 1.3 g fiber per serving   2 servings

INGREDIENTS:

- 2 cups sliced baby bella mushrooms
- 1 cup sliced leeks
- 1/2 cup chicken broth or white wine
- sea salt
- pepper

DIRECTIONS:

Heat a large sauté pan over medium heat. Use a light coating of cooking spray. Add mushrooms and salt and pepper. Cook down for 5 minutes before adding leeks. Add the cooking liquid, and cook until the liquid has evaporated. Check to see if it needs more salt and pepper before serving.

LEEKS NEED TO BE WASHED REALLY WELL to remove any dirt. Slice and soak in water before cooking.

A LIGHT VERSION OF COCONUT RICE, but still full of flavor and decadence.

Great as a side dish or a sweet dessert.

COCONUT RICE
210 calories, 31 g protein, 13 g carbs, 5 g fat, 2 g fiber   4 - 1/2 cup servings

INGREDIENTS:

- 1 cup uncooked brown rice
- 2 cups coconut water
- 1/4 cup lite coconut milk
- dried unsweetened coconut, shredded
- sea salt

DIRECTIONS:

Cook the rice as directed on the package using a rice cooker or on the stovetop. In place of water use the coconut water. Once rice is cooked, heat a skillet over medium high heat. Add cooked rice and coconut milk. Mix, and press into a thin layer in the skillet so it can caramelize. Allow to sit for a few minutes, stir and press down again to allow for more caramelization. Sprinkle with sea salt to taste and garnish with shredded coconut.

ASIAN CARROT AND JICAMA SLAW

80 calories, 1 g protein, 15.5 g carb, 1.25 g fat, 3.5 g fiber   4 servings

INGREDIENTS:

- 1 medium carrot about 135 g, shredded
- about 1/4 of a jicama, or 135 g, shredded
- cups cabbage, or 135 g, shredded
- fresh sliced scallion to garnish

DRESSING INGREDIENTS:

- 1/2 cup coconut aminos
- 2 tbsp rice vinegar
- 1 tsp sesame oil
- 1 tbsp swerve or preferred sweetener
- 1/2 tbsp Korean chili flakes (gochugaru)
- 1 tsp minced ginger
- 1 tsp minced garlic

DIRECTIONS:

Combine the shredded carrot, jicama, and cabbage.

To prepare the dressing, I always use a jar to shake it up and to seal and store the leftovers. Combine all ingredients for the dressing. Toss the dressing with the slaw until well combined. Garnish with fresh scallions.

IF YOU'RE NOT FAMILIAR with jicama, it's similar to a water chestnut in texture. It has a lot of fiber and a high water content. Common in Mexican cooking, it looks like a funny shaped potato and must be peeled. The skin is inedible.

CREAMY ZUCCHINI

140 calories, 13.8 g protein, 17 g carbs, 1.5 g fat, 3.35 g fiber   4 servings

INGREDIENTS:

- 2 medium zucchinis, diced into uniform pieces
- 1/4 cup fat free cream cheese
- sea salt
- pepper

DIRECTIONS:

Heat a large skillet over medium high heat. Coat the pan with a quick spray of non-stick cooking spray.

Add diced zucchini, spread evenly to get a good sear. Toss a few times to get some color on all sides. about 5 minutes total cooking time, or to desired tenderness.

Once the zucchini is done cooking add the cream cheese to the hot pan and toss until melted. Sprinkle with sea salt and pepper.

SAUCES AND SEASONINGS

Sweet chile sauce

Thai peanut sauce

Korean BBQ marinade

Balsamic reduction

Sweet mustard

Moroccan mustard

Chive pesto

Vanilla glaze

Mustard rub/seasoning

SWEET CHILE SAUCE

60 calories, 1.4 g protein, 17 g carbs, 0 g fat, 3.2 g fiber   2 servings

INGREDIENTS:

- 3 tbsp strawberry jam, sugar free
- 1/2 cup vinegar
- 1 tbsp coconut nectar or agave nectar
- 1 tsp cayenne pepper
- 1 tbsp chopped peppers, red jalapeños
- 1 tbsp fish sauce
- 1 tbsp coconut aminos
- 4 garlic cloves, minced

DIRECTIONS:

Combine all ingredients in a small sautée pan and heat over medium high heat. Bring to a low boil and reduce to a simmer for 5 minutes. Remove from heat and allow to cool before serving.

THAI PEANUT SAUCE

17 calories, .8 g protein, 4.6 g carbs, 0 g fat, 2.9 g fiber   4 servings

INGREDIENTS:

- 1 tbsp powdered peanut butter
- 3 tbsp water
- 1-2 tsp crushed red pepper
- 1 tbsp VitaFiber
- 1 tsp tomato paste
- 1/2 tbsp hoisin
- 1 stevia packet

DIRECTIONS:

Mix all ingredients together in a small resealable container.

KOREAN BBQ MARINADE AND DIPPING SAUCE

Marinade: 40 calories, .6 g protein, 9.3 g carbs, 0 g fat, .8 g fiber   4 servings
Sauce: 66 calories, .35 g protein, 9.5 g carbs, 3 g fat, 1 g fiber

MARINADE INGREDIENTS:

- 1 cup coconut aminos
- 3 tbsp strawberry jam, sugar free
- 1 tbsp chili paste "sambal"
- 2 tbsp ginger, fresh grated
- 6 garlic cloves
- 2 tbsp white wine vinegar or rice vinegar
- 1 stevia packet

DIPPING SAUCE INGREDIENTS:

- 1/2 of reserved marinade
- 2 tsp sesame oil
- black pepper
- 1/2 tbsp sesame seeds
- 1 green onion, sliced

DIRECTIONS FOR MARINADE:

Combine all of the marinade ingredients in bowl. Reserve half to make the dipping sauce. Use to marinate chicken or beef at least an hour or overnight.

DIRECTIONS FOR SAUCE:

To the reserved marinade add the remaining ingredients, stir, and serve.

BALSAMIC REDUCTION

28 calories, .2 g protein, 5.4 g carbs, 0 g fat, 0 g fiber   per 1 tbsp serving

INGREDIENTS:

- 1 cup balsamic vinegar
- 1 tsp stevia (swerve)

DIRECTIONS:

Bring to boil and reduce to simmer until the vinegar is reduced by half

SWEET MUSTARD

19 calories, 0 g protein, 2 g carbs, 1 g fat, 0 g fiber   per tablespoon

INGREDIENTS:

- 1/3 cup whole grain mustard
- 3 tbsp sugar-free jam (strawberry or apricot)

DIRECTIONS:

Combine ingredients and store in an air-tight container.

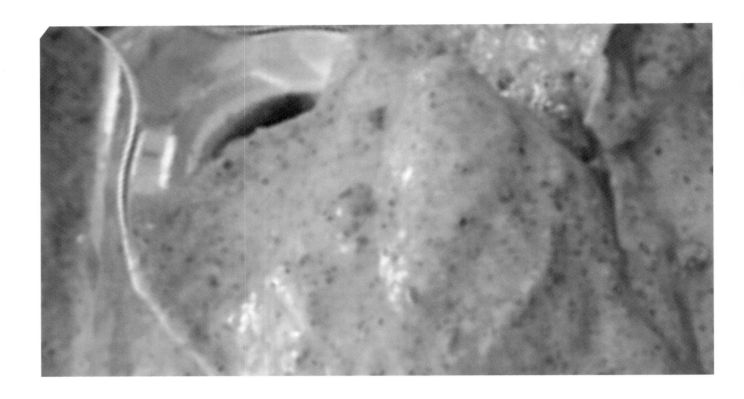

MOROCCAN MUSTARD

14 calories, 0 g protein, <1 g carbs, <1 g fat, 0 g fiber   per tablespoon

This recipe is perfect for marinating 1 lb of chicken.

INGREDIENTS:

- 50 g or 1/3 cup Dijon mustard
- 1 tsp ras el hanout spice blend
- 1 tsp sumac
- 1 tsp Aleppo pepper

DIRECTIONS:

Mix all ingredients together in a small resealable container.

I'M NOT REALLY A MUSTARD FAN, BUT I LOVE THIS!

It's a super low-calorie condiment. Use it as a dip for a crudité platter, or as a marinade for chicken.

Ras el hanout is a North African spice blend. These spices are becoming more common, but if you cannot find them in the spice section of the grocery store they are easily found online. They are inexpensive and the flavors are unique and addictive.

CHIVE PESTO

35 calories, 0 g protein, 0 g carbs, 4 g fat, 0 g fiber   per 1 tsp serving

INGREDIENTS:

- 4 tbsp olive oil
- 1 bunch chives, about 18 g, roughly chopped

DIRECTIONS:

Combine in a food processor or blender until smooth.

DEPENDING ON THE BLENDER or food processor you use, you may need to make a larger batch so the blades can adequately blend the ingredients.

VANILLA GLAZE

8 calories, 0 g protein, 2 g carbs, 0 g fat, 0 g fiber   1 serving

IINGREDIENTS:

- 1 tbsp powdered swerve
- 1/2 tsp vanilla bean paste
- 1/2 tbsp water

GREAT ON DESSERTS or savory dishes!

DIRECTIONS:

Mix all ingredients until smooth.

PERFECT FOR A RUB on chicken or pork.

Add a punch of flavor to veggies or salad dressing.

MUSTARD RUB/SEASONING
62 calories, 4.2 g protein, 8 g carbs, 2.3 g fat, 1.5 g fiber   12 servings

INGREDIENTS:

- 1/4 cup dry mustard
- 1 tsbp swerve sweetener
- 1 tsp sea salt
- 1 tsp cayenne pepper

DIRECTIONS:

Combine ingredients in an air tight container. This recipe makes enough to season 2 lbs of chicken.

DESSERTS

BCAA gelatin snacks

Doughnuts

Cookie dough

Snickerdoodles

Frozen peanut butter cups

Gingerbread cookies

Brownies

Zucchini bread

Pumpkin pie ice cream

Goat cheese icing

Cream cheese icing

Kabocha gingerbread cake

Chocolate chip peanut butter protein bars

Protein crispy bars

Chocolate sauce

Lemon cream pudding

Guilt free angel food cake

Let there be cheesecake!

Zucchini brownies

Snickerdoodle cake

Pumpkin cheesecake

Double chocolate chip cake

THIS IS A GREAT LOW-CALORIE SNACK.
It'll satisfy a sweet tooth and help to maintain muscle between meals especially when you are dieting.

My kids love these! I can't keep them in the house!

BCAA GELATIN SNACKS
12 calories, 3 g protein, 0 g carbs, 0 g fat, 0 g fiber

8 servings

INGREDIENTS:

- 4 packets of gelatin
- 2 cups cold water
- 2 cups boiling water
- 4 scoops flavored BCAAs

DIRECTIONS:

In a 9 x 13 glass baking dish combine cold water, gelatin, and BCAAs. Allow the gelatin to bloom in the water for 5 minutes. While the gelatin is soaking, heat the remaining 2 cups water in a saucepan just until it boils. Slowly add it to the gelatin mixture and stir until it begins to thicken slightly. Cover and refrigerate until it sets.

WHAT ARE BCAAs? Branch chain amino acids are the building block of protein. As a sports supplement they come in a variety of flavors and they are sugar and calorie free. They do oftentimes add electrolytes and glutamine for recovery. Flavors to look for are lemon-lime, orange, mango, apple, grape, strawberry kiwi, watermelon, and blue raspberry.

GLAZED DOUGHNUTS

80 calories per doughnut, 7.8 g protein, 7.8 g carbs, 3 g fat, 6.4 g fiber   6 doughnuts

INGREDIENTS:

- 1 egg and 1 egg white
- 1/2 cup almond milk
- 1/2 cup canned cannellini beans
- 1 tsp vanilla
- 1/2 cup vanilla protein blend
- 2 tbsp almond meal
- 2 tbsp coconut flour
- 1/2 tsp baking powder
- 1/4 tsp sea salt
- 1/2 tsp baking soda
- 1/2 tsp freshly grated nutmeg
- 1/3 cup Splenda

CHOCOLATE GLAZE:

- 2 tbsp VitaFiber
- 1 tbsp water
- 1 tbsp cocoa powder

DIRECTIONS:

Preheat oven to 350 degrees F. Combine eggs, almond milk, beans, and vanilla in a blender or food processor. Mix until all of the beans have been pureed and the mixture is smooth. In another bowl combine the rest of the dry ingredients and whisk. Combine the wet and dry ingredients either in the food processor or the bowl and mix. There is no gluten so you don't have to worry about over-mixing. Lightly coat a doughnut pan with cooking spray (you can also use a muffin tin). There should be enough batter to make six doughnuts. Bake in the oven for 12 minutes. Allow to cool and carefully remove from the pan. Combine all ingredients for chocolate glaze and drizzle over doughnuts.

TOO GOOD TO BE TRUE!

Light and fluffy with a rich chocolate sauce. Try them coated in cinnamon and stevia or with a vanilla glaze. To make the glaze mix vanilla, powdered swerve, and a tiny bit of water to thin it out.

COOKIE DOUGH

115 calories, 8 g protein, 16.3 g carbs, 3 g fat, 4.25 g fiber

8 servings, 70 g per serving

INGREDIENTS:

- 1 can garbanzo beans
- 1/2 cup or 100 g swerve sweetener
- 4 oz. fat-free cream cheese
- 1 scoop vanilla whey protein or protein blend
- 2 tbsp coconut flour
- 1/4 tsp sea salt
- 1/3 cup or 65 g stevia-sweetened chocolate chips

DIRECTIONS:

In a food processor or blender combine everything except for the chocolate chips and puree until smooth. Scoop out the dough and mix in the chocolate chips. Store in a resealable container. This is intended to be eaten raw since there are no eggs, but it can also be baked into cookies.

SNICKERDOODLES

68 calories per cookie, 3.3 g protein, 2 g carbs, 6 g fat, 2 g fiber   14 cookies

INGREDIENTS:

- 1/4 cup coconut oil
- 1/4 cup fat-free Greek yogurt
- 1cup Splenda
- 1 egg (64 g)
- 47 g whey, or 1/2 cup
- 1/4 cup coconut flour
- 1/4 cup almond flour
- 1/2 tsp baking powder
- 1/4 tsp salt
- 1 tbsp konjac flour
- 1 tsp vanilla butter / nut flavor

DIRECTIONS:

Preheat the oven to 350 degrees F. In a medium sized mixing bowl or using a stand mixer combine melted coconut oil, yogurt, Splenda or sugar of choice, egg, and mix to combine. In another bowl add the remaining dry ingredients and mix well. Add the dry ingredients to the wet, slowly mixing as you go. Roll pieces of dough into bite sized balls and place on a cookie sheet with cooking spray or parchment paper. Press the dough balls flat leaving about 1/2 inch between cookies. Bake for 10-12 minutes. Watch them so they don't burn.

KONJAC FLOUR,
also known as glucomannan, is a low-calorie high-fiber flour. It has been used for centuries in Japan. It absorbs 200 times its weight in liquid, so a little goes a long way. Because it is high in fiber it makes you feel full longer and adds low-calorie bulk to a recipe.

It is what shirataki noodles are made of, and you can buy the flour on its own to use in your own recipes.

A GREAT POP OF CHOCOLATE
when the craving arises. The kids love 'em!

The nutrition facts may vary based on the protein powder that you use.

FROZEN PEANUT BUTTER CUPS

210 calories, 31 g protein, 13 g carbs, 5 g fat, 2 g fiber

This recipe makes 1 serving, which should fill about 6 cubes depending on your tray.
AS A SNACK: 35 calories per cube, 5 g protein, 2 g carbs, .8 g fat, .3 g fiber

INGREDIENTS:

- 1 scoop chocolate or vanilla whey protein powder
- 1 tsp unsweetened cocoa powder (optional)
- 1/4 cup powdered peanut butter
- 1/2 cup water, divided
- silicon or regular ice cube tray (the silicon tray is easier to unmold)

DIRECTIONS:

Mix the protein powder with 1/4 cup of water until it's a pudding-like consistency. Add the cocoa powder if you like a richer chocolaty flavor and some stevia if needed (depends on the protein powder you use). Fill the mold halfway and freeze for about 30 minutes just until it's starting to set. Add a little bit of water to the powdered protein until it gets to a pudding glide consistency and fill the molds the rest of the way. Should set in a few hours and they are ready to pop out and enjoy. Allow to sit out for a minute to soften before chowing down.

GINGERBREAD COOKIES

39 calories per cookie, 2.2 g protein, 27 g carbs, 2 g fat, 25 g fiber 12–14 cookies

INGREDIENTS:

- 2 cups Carbquik flour
- 2 tsp cinnamon
- 1/8 tsp ground cloves
- 1/4 tsp ground nutmeg
- 1/4 tsp sea salt
- 1/4 tsp baking powder
- 1/4 tsp baking soda
- a few grinds of black pepper
- 1 tbsp molasses
- 1 extra large egg
- 1 to 1.5 tbsp grated ginger
- 1/2 cup sugar-free maple syrup
- 1 tsp vanilla
- 1/4 cup swerve granulated sweetener

TOPPING INGREDIENTS:

- 1/4 cup swerve powdered sweetener*
- 1 tbsp water

DIRECTIONS:

Preheat the oven to 350 degrees F. In a medium-sized bowl combine the first eight dry ingredients, stopping at the molasses, and mix to combine. In another bowl combine the rest of the wet ingredients. Add the wet to the dry ingredients and mix well. Spoon dough onto a parchment-lined baking sheet and bake for 8 minutes. Allow to cool. Combine the powdered swerve and water mix and drizzle over cookies.

GINGERBREAD COOKIES are probably one of my favorite desserts, especially around the holidays. I needed to find something that would satisfy my craving without sabotaging my caloric intake for the day.

BROWNIES

77.5 calories, 8.2 g protein, 6.4 g carbs, 2.3 g fat, 2.4 g fiber per bar   9 servings

INGREDIENTS:

- 1/3 cup swerve sweetener
- 119 g egg whites (3 egg whites)
- 1 approx. 400 g eggplant (about the length of your hand in size)
- 1 tsp vanilla
- 75 g chocolate whey protein
- 1/4 cup cocoa powder
- 1 tbsp black cocoa
- stevia chocolate chips 40 g

DIRECTIONS:

Preheat oven to 350 degrees F. Pierce the eggplant all over and place in a microwave-safe dish. Microwave for about 4 minutes until soft. When it's cool enough to handle slice off the top and scoop out the flesh. In a bowl or the food processor add all of the ingredients and blend. Coat a 2 qt. baking dish with cooking spray. Pour the batter in and bake for 30 minutes, until a toothpick inserted in the center comes out clean. Be careful not to overbake (whey protein can become rubbery if overcooked).

EGGPLANT IN BROWNIES?
I know it may sound strange, but it adds no flavor and tons of moisture. It's a great way to sneak those veggies into your kids.

THIS BREAD MAKES
a great snack when you just
need something sweet!

A great way to sneak some veggies and fiber into my kids too!

CHOCOLATE CHIP ZUCCHINI BREAD
93 calories, 10.25 g protein, 29 g carbs, 3.5 g fat, 21 g fiber   12 servings

INGREDIENTS:

- 2 egg whites
- 1 tsp vanilla
- 1/3 cup swerve 77 g
- 1/3 cup sugar-free maple syrup
- 1.5 cups Carbquik flour
- 1 cup (122 g) cinnamon bun or unflavored protein powder
- 1/2 tsp baking powder
- 1 tsp baking soda
- 1 tsp cinnamon
- 1/2 tsp nutmeg
- 1/4 tsp salt
- 428 g zucchini (2 medium)
- 65 g stevia chocolate chips (Lily's)

DIRECTIONS:

Preheat the oven to 350 degrees F. Combine egg whites, vanilla, and swerve in a stand mixer and beat until its light and fluffy, about 5 minutes. While the egg and sugar mixture is beating, combine the dry ingredients (except for the chocolate chips) in a mixing bowl. Grate the zucchini and add it to the egg mixture along with the maple syrup. Slowly add the dry ingredients. Lightly coat the chocolate chips with a little bit of flour and, once combined, stir them into the mixture. Lightly spray a loaf pan with cooking spray and pour in the batter. Bake for 35–40 minutes, until a toothpick comes out clean. Allow to cool on a cooling rack. Once it's cool enough to remove from the loaf pan, slice and serve

PUMPKIN ICE CREAM WITH ZUCCHINI BREAD AND GOAT CHEESE ICING

Substitute fat-free cream cheese icing for a lighter version, but just as tasty.

Cream cheese has a milder flavor than goat cheese.

SWEET POTATO AND APPLE ICE CREAM

135 calories, 2.5 g protein, 23 g carbs, 3.8 g fat, 2.7g fiber   6 servings

INGREDIENTS:

- 8 oz. silken tofu
- 1 cup unsweetened almond milk
- 8 oz. baked yam skin, removed
- 1 granny smith apple (about 5 oz.) peeled
- 1/4 cup Splenda, swerve or stevia
- 1 tsp vanilla
- 1 tsp xanthan gum
- 1 tbsp coconut oil melted
- 2 tsp pumpkin pie spice
- 1 tsp cinnamon
- a few grinds of black pepper
- 1/4 cup sugar-free maple syrup

DIRECTIONS:

Combine all ingredients in a food processor until thick and creamy. Allow to chill for a few hours to make sure it is very cold. Making sure the mixture is very cold will ensure a creamier texture. Put in an ice cream maker until it reaches a soft serve consistency. Serve immediately or freeze for a bit to harden if you prefer that texture. Serve with chocolate chip zucchini bread topped with cream cheese frosting for a decadent dessert!

GOAT CHEESE ICING

56 calories, 3 g protein, 2.75 g carbs, 4 g fat, 0 g fiber   4 servings

INGREDIENTS:

- 57 g or 2 oz. goat cheese
- 2 stevia packets
- 1 tsp vanilla; paste is preferred

DIRECTIONS:

Combine all ingredients until creamy.

CREAM CHEESE ICING

18.75 calories, 2 g protein, 1.5 g carbs, <1 g fat, 0 g fiber   4 servings

INGREDIENTS:

- 57 g or 2 oz. fat-free cream cheese
- 2 stevia packets
- 1 tsp vanilla; paste is preferred

DIRECTIONS:

Combine all ingredients until creamy.

KABOCHA GINGERBREAD CAKE

52 calories, 3 g protein, 25 g carbs,1 g fat, 18 g fiber   9 servings

INGREDIENTS:

- 1 kabocha squash
- 2 egg whites
- 2 tsp vanilla
- 1/2 cup swerve
- 1/2 tsp baking powder
- 3 tsp ginger, fresh grated or ground
- 3 tsp cinnamon, ground
- 1/4 tsp cloves, ground
- 1/2 tsp nutmeg, fresh grated
- 1 tsp salt
- 1/2 cup maple syrup
- 1/2 cup unsweetened almond milk
- 1 cup Carbquik baking mix

DIRECTIONS:

To prepare the squash cut in half and remove the seeds. Bake in oven 25–30 minutes at 350 degrees F. Place cut side down on a baking sheet. Bake until tender. Allow to cool and scoop out the flesh.

In an electric mixer mix the egg whites, vanilla, and swerve and blend until fluffy, about 5 minutes.

While the eggs and sugar a mixing combine the dry ingredients—Carbquick, baking powder, ginger, cinnamon, cloves, nutmeg, salt. Set aside.

To the egg mixture, add the squash, almond milk, maple syrup. Mix .

Slowly add the dry mixture to the wet. In a square 8 x 8 or 9 x 9 baking pan coated with cooking spray add the batter. Bake in oven at 350 degrees F about 35 minutes, until a toothpick inserted into the center comes out clean. Allow to cool and top with vanilla glaze.

CHOCOLATE MARBLE PEANUT BUTTER BARS

196 calories, 19.25 g protein, 25 g carb, 6.9 g fat, 16.75 g fiber   2 servings

INGREDIENTS:

- 3 tbsp VitaFiber syrup
- 1.5 scoops whey protein (use your favorite flavor)
- 1 tbsp powdered peanut butter (optional)
- stevia packet (depending on the sweetness of your protein)
- 30 g stevia chocolate chips
- pinch of sea salt

DIRECTIONS:

Heat the VitaFiber in a small sauce pan just until it starts a light boil. Remove from heat and stir in the protein powder and powdered peanut butter if using it. I use a peanut butter–flavored protein powder but any will work. Add the stevia if you want added sweetness. Mix quickly until combined. Using a zip top lunch-sized baggie, fold the edges over so it doesn't get messy on the outside. At the last minute fold in the chocolate chips. The mixture is hot, so if you add them too early it will all melt together. Place the whole mixture in the plastic baggie, flatten it out, seal it, and allow to chill in the refrigerator. It will harden and you can cut it into bars. It will get pretty hard when cold, so allow to sit out for a few minutes to soften before eating.

HIGH FIBER AND HIGH PROTEIN
make these bars ideal for even the strictest of diets.

Switch it up by trying different flavored protein powder. My favorites are peanut butter and chocolate.

THESE LOW-CALORIE HIGH-FIBER BARS ARE SO DELICIOUS. My kids love them.

Just like the real thing with none of the guilt!

CRISPY FIBER BARS

101.5 calories, 3.8 g protein, 30 g carbs, 1.5 g fat, 12.3 g fiber   4 servings

INGREDIENTS:

- 100 g VitaFiber
- 1 cup Rice Krispies
- 1/4 cup Fiber One
- 14 g stevia chocolate chips
- 1/2 scoop whey protein
- sea salt
- 1 stevia packet

DIRECTIONS:

In a small sauce pan heat the VitaFiber just until bubbly. Remove from the heat and stir in the stevia, and the protein powder. Once combined, mix in the cereals. Add the chocolate chips (if it's too warm they will melt; it still tastes good, but if you want them in chips wait for it to cool a bit). Spread evenly in a small pan and top with sea salt. Allow to chill in the fridge to set up.

CHOCOLATE GANACHE

80 calories, 1 g protein, 32 g carbs, <1 g fat, 31.8 g fiber

1 serving

INGREDIENTS:

- 1 tbsp cocoa powder
- 1 tbsp water
- 2 tbsp VitaFiber

DIRECTIONS:

Mix all ingredients together until well combined.

THE CARBOHYDRATES ALL COME FROM FIBER so it's low calorie and has zero sugar and almost no fat!

You can change it up by using different cocoa powders like red or black cocoa.

Excellent as a healthy topping for ice cream.

SUPER LIGHT AND CREAMY.

Great for an easy low-cal sweet snack for the whole family.

LEMON CREAM PUDDING
25 calories, 1.75 g protein, .7 g carbs, 1.8 g fat, .4 g fiber   4 servings

INGREDIENTS:

- 1.4 oz. package of sugar-free lemon Jell-O
- 1 tsp vanilla bean paste
- unsweetened almond milk

DIRECTIONS:

Prepare the pudding per package instructions using unsweetened almond milk instead of water in the recipe. Mix in the vanilla and pour into individual serving cups and chill in the refrigerator to set.

GUILT FREE ANGEL FOOD CAKE

129 calories, 21.4 g protein, 8 g carbs, 1.25 g fat, 1.25 g fiber   4 servings

1 serving = 1/4 of the cake or 120 g

INGREDIENTS:

- 12 egg whites or 442 g, at room temperature
- 2 tsp cream of tartar
- 1/2 cup swerve 86 g
- 1 tsp vanilla extract
- 1 tsp almond extract
- 1.5 scoops whey protein or 56 g (I like protolyte pancakes and syrup flavor in this recipe)
- 1/2 tsp sea salt
- 1 tsp glucomannan

DIRECTIONS:

Preheat the oven to 300 degrees F with the angel food cake pan in the oven. Begin to beat the egg whites with an electric mixer with the whisk attachment. Gradually add the cream of tartar. Then add the vanilla and almond extracts. Beat until the mixture has stiff peaks. Do not over beat.

Combine the remaining ingredients in a separate bowl and sprinkle them gently over the top of the egg white mixture. Fold gently with a spatula. Remove the pan from the oven and pour the batter in. *DO NOT USE cooking spray.

Before placing the cake in the oven, turn it down to 275 degrees. Bake for 65 minutes without opening the oven door. Once baked, turn upside down over a bottle to cool. This will keep the cake from collapsing. Once cool, remove from the pan. You may need to loosen it with a butter knife. Your oven may vary with the cooking time, so it may take some experimentation to get it right. The top will be golden and may begin to crack.

HIGH IN PROTEIN, LOW IN CARBS.
No flour, no guilt. The kids love this cake, too!

Do not use pasteurized egg whites from the carton.

LET THERE BE CHEESECAKE!

118 calories, 12 g protein, 16 g carb, 1.8 g fat, 4 g fiber   per 111 g slice

CRUST INGREDIENTS:

- 1/2 cup fiber cereal 31 g
- 1/2 cup graham cracker crumbs 50 g
- VitaFiber syrup 40 g

FILLING INGREDIENTS:

- 16 oz. fat free cream cheese, softened
- 1/2 cup swerve sweetener 100 g
- 1/4 tsp sea salt
- 1 tsp vanilla
- 1 egg + 3 egg whites

TOPPING:

- 1 container fat free vanilla greek yogurt (80 calories) 150 g
- 1 tbsp unsweetened almond milk or water

DIRECTIONS:

Preheat the oven to 350 degrees F. Begin by preparing the crust. Combine the crust ingredients in a 9" spring form pan. Press the crust into the bottom of the pan evenly. Wrap the outside of the pan with foil. This is baked in the oven in a water bath, so this ensures no water will leak into the cake. Allow to chill while preparing the other ingredients.

To prepare the filling. using an electric mixer, combine the cream cheese and sugar until light and fluffy. Add the remaining ingredients until well combined scraping the sides a few times. Pour over the prepared crust. To make the water bath, place the foil lined cake pan into a roasting pan and fill with water so it is about 1 inch up the outside of the cake pan. Bake in the oven for 50 minutes.

Once the cake has cooled. combine the yogurt and a little bit of almond milk or water to thin slightly, spread over the top of the cake.

ZUCCHINI BROWNIES

62 calories, 4.2 g protein, 8 g carbs, 2.3 g fat, 1.5 g fiber per brownie   12 servings

INGREDIENTS:

- 2 medium zucchini (about 348 g)
- 1 egg + 3 egg whites
- 1/2 cup swerve sweetener 100 g
- 1 single serving non-fat greek yogurt plain (150 g)
- 42 g or 1/2 cup unsweetened cocoa powder
- 1 tsp vanilla
- 1/4 tsp sea salt
- 1 scoop chocolate whey protein (about 35 g)
- 50 g stevia chocolate chips (Lily's brand)

DIRECTIONS:

Preheat the oven to 350 degrees. Begin by cutting the raw zucchini into chunks and puree in a large cup food processor. Once it is a fine puree add the remaining ingredients except for the chocolate chips and process to combine. Using a spatula stir in the chocolate chips.

Coat an 11" x 7" or a square baking pan with non-stick spray and pour in the batter.

Bake for 30 minutes. It will start to crack at the top, but a toothpick inserted in the center will not come out clean. They will have a fudge like texture.

I KNOW IT MAY SOUND a little odd, but it's a great way to sneak some veggies into your kids' food.

No flour, gluten free, low fat and low carb. Great with some low fat ice cream!

LIGHT, FLUFFY, LOW CARB, low fat, and high protein.

Serve alone, with vanilla yogurt, or some light ice cream.

SNICKERDOODLE CAKE
84 calories, 13 g protein, 4 g carbs, 1 g fat, 0 g fiber

6 servings,
75 g per serving

WET INGREDIENTS:

- 4 oz. fat free cream cheese
- 1/2 cup or 100 g swerve sweetener
- 1 tbsp vanilla
- 1 egg + 2 egg whites

WET INGREDIENTS:

- 2 scoops whey isolate protein
- 1 tsp baking soda
- 1/4 tsp sea salt
- 1/2 tsp cinnamon

TOPPING:

- 1 tbsp swerve
- 1/2 tsp cinnamon

DIRECTIONS:

Preheat the oven to 350 degrees. In a mixer cream the cream cheese and the sugar until light and fluffy. Add the remaining wet ingredients and mix until combined. In a separate bowl add the dry ingredients and mix. Add them to the wet ingredients and mix to combine. Pour the batter in a baking pan coated with non-stick spray. Combine the topping ingredients and sprinkle over the batter. Bake for 15 minutes.

PUMPKIN CHEESECAKE

127 calories, 12.4 g protein, 17.8 g carbs, 1.8 g fat, 4 g fiber

8 servings,
122 g per serving

CRUST INGREDIENTS:

- 1/2 cup fiber cereal 31g
- 1/2 cup graham cracker crumbs 50 g
- 1 tbsp swerve sweetener
- VitaFiber syrup 40 g

FILLING INGREDIENTS:

- 16oz. fat free cream cheese, softened
- 1/2 cup + 1 tbsp swerve sweetener 105 g
- 1/4 tsp sea salt
- 1 tsp vanilla
- 1/2 cup pumpkin puree, unsweetened
- 1 tsp pumpkin pie spice
- 1 egg + 3 egg whites

TOPPING:

- 1 container fat free vanilla greek yogurt (80 calories) 150 g
- 1 tbsp unsweetened almond milk or water

DIRECTIONS:

Preheat the oven to 350 degrees F. Begin by preparing the crust. Combine the crust ingredients in a 9" spring form pan. Press the crust into the bottom of the pan evenly. Wrap the outside of the pan with foil. This is baked in the oven in a water bath, so this ensures no water will leak into the cake. Allow to chill while preparing the other ingredients.

To prepare the filling: Using an electric mixer, combine the cream cheese and sugar until light and fluffy. Add the remaining ingredients until well combined scraping the sides a few times. Pour over the prepared crust. To make the water bath, place the foil lined cake pan into a roasting pan and fill with water so it is about 1 inch up the outside of the cake pan. Bake in the oven for 50 minutes.

Once the cake has cooled, combine the yogurt and a little bit of almond milk or water to thin slightly, spread over the top of the cake.

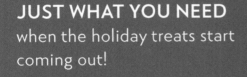

JUST WHAT YOU NEED
when the holiday treats start coming out!

DOUBLE CHOCOLATE CHIP CAKE

184 calories, 23 g protein, 13 g carbs, 5 g fat, 2 g fiber

Serving size is 1/4 of the cake

INGREDIENTS:

- 12 egg whites or 442 g, at room temperature
- 2 tsp cream of tartar
- 1 tsp vanilla extract
- 1 tsp almond extract
- 1/2 cup swerve 86 g
- 1.5 scoops whey protein or 56 g (I like protolyte pancakes and syrup flavor in this recipe)
- 1/2 tsp sea salt
- 1 tsp glucomannan
- 50 g stevia chocolate chips (Lily's)

DIRECTIONS:

Preheat the oven to 300 degrees F with the angel food cake pan in the oven. Begin to beat the egg whites with an electric mixer with the whisk attachment. Gradually add the cream of tartar. Then add the vanilla and almond extracts. Beat until the mixture has stiff peaks. Do not over beat.

Combine the remaining ingredients in a separate bowl and sprinkle them gently over the top of the egg white mixture. Fold gently with a spatula. Remove the pan from the oven and pour the batter in. *DO NOT USE cooking spray.

Before placing the cake in the oven, turn it down to 275 degrees. Bake for 65 minutes without opening the oven door. Once baked, turn upside down over a bottle to cool. This will keep the cake from collapsing. Once cool, remove from the pan. You may need to loosen it with a butter knife. Your oven may vary with the cooking time, so it may take some experimentation to get it right. The top will be golden and may begin to crack.

DECADENT AND RICH, A STAPLE IN MY HOUSE. Great for a healthy dessert anytime or a special occasion treat.

Yes! A serving is 1/4 of the cake so you can eat a huge chunk with no guilt.

DRINKS

Infused water

Mocha slushy

Strawberry basil slushy

Jalapeño lime slushy

Hot mocha

INFUSED WATER
is a great way to add calorie-free natural flavor to your water.

INFUSED WATER
0 calories, 0 g protein, 0 g carbs, 0 g fat, 0 g fiber

INGREDIENT COMBINATIONS:

- strawberry and cucumber
- cantaloupe
- mint and lime
- ginger and peach
- pineapple and mint
- strawberry and basil

DIRECTIONS:

Combine your favorite fruits, veggies and herbs in a pitcher and allow to chill in the fridge for at least an hour to get the flavors infused.

MOCHA SLUSHY

153 calories, 24.3 g protein, 8.3 g carbs, 5 g fat, 1.3 g fiber   1 serving

INGREDIENTS:

- 1 scoop chocolate whey protein powder
- stevia to taste
- 1/2 cup crushed ice
- 1 1/2 cup water or unsweetened almond milk
- 1 tbsp cocoa powder
- 1 tsp to 1 tbsp instant coffee or espresso to taste
- 1 tsp chopped coco nibs (optional)

DIRECTIONS:

Combine all ingredients in a blender and blend until smooth.

A RICH CHOCOLATE COFFEEHOUSE-STYLE PROTEIN SHAKE.
Great for a sweet treat or breakfast on the go.

Guilt free and super tasty.

STRAWBERRY, BASIL, AND BLACK PEPPER

are among my favorite flavor combinations. Don't let the pepper scare you. Trust me, it's delicious!

I love pepper in sweet applications. It's such a nice surprise! Just like adding salt to a dessert, it creates balance.

STRAWBERRY BASIL SLUSHY
16 calories, 2 g protein, 2 g carbs, 5 g fat, 0 g fiber   1 serving

INGREDIENTS:

- 1 tsp strawberry flavored sugar-free drink mix or BCAAs
- a few fresh basil leaves
- a few grinds of black pepper
- 1 1/2 cups crushed ice
- 2 cups water
- 1 tsp powdered glutamine (optional)
- 1/2 tbsp powdered collagen

DIRECTIONS:

Combine all ingredients in a blender and blend until smooth.

STRAWBERRY JALAPEÑO SLUSHY

16 calories, 2 g protein, 2 g carbs, 0 g fat, fiber   1 serving

INGREDIENTS:

- 1 tsp strawberry flavored sugar-free drink mix or strawberry flavored BCAAs
- a slice of fresh jalapeño, to taste (remove seeds and ribs to reduce heat)
- squeeze of fresh lime juice
- 1 1/2 cups crushed ice
- 2 cups water
- 1 tsp powdered glutamine (optional)
- 1/2 tbsp powdered collagen

DIRECTIONS:

Combine all ingredients in a blender and blend until smooth.

THE GLUTAMINE AND COLLAGEN ARE NOT ONLY beneficial for repairing hair, skin, nails, joints, tendons, and ligaments, they are great for texture and smoothness in all my slushy drinks. I also add them to shakes and smoothies.

I PREFER TO USE VANILLA BEAN PASTE for just about everything I use vanilla for. It is made with seeds scraped from the pod, so you get an authentic "French" vanilla taste.

ORANGE DREAM SLUSHY

22 calories, 2 g protein, 3 g carbs, 0 g fat, 0 g fiber   1 serving

INGREDIENTS:

- 1 tsp orange flavored sugar-free drink mix or orange flavored BCAAs
- 1 tsp of vanilla or vanilla bean paste
- 1 1/2 cups crushed ice
- 2 cups water
- 1 tsp powdered glutamine (optional)
- 1/2 tbsp powdered collagen

DIRECTIONS:

Combine all ingredients in a blender and blend until smooth.

HOT MOCHA

123 calories, 23 g protein, 3 g carbs, 2 g fat, 0 g fiber   1 serving
(nutrition facts may vary depending on protein powder)

INGREDIENTS:

- 1.5 cups hot coffee
- stevia to taste
- 1/2 to 1 scoop of chocolate protein powder

DIRECTIONS:

Brew coffee and add stevia. If you add the protein powder when it is too hot it will get chunky. You can add a few ice cubes or some cool water to lower the temperature. Once the coffee is slightly cooled, but still hot, add the protein powder, mix, and enjoy.

I DRINK THIS EVERY MORNING.

It makes me feel like I'm having a rich mocha from a coffee shop. Plus I get a boost of protein first thing in the morning.

If you like creamer, almond milk and cashew milk are a great low cal addition.

I WANT YOU TO SUCCEED!

Check out FITSTARTSINTHEKITCHEN.COM for support. There you will have access to training plans for all levels as well as nutrition articles, videos, recipes, and Q&A with me. You can create a personal profile so I can get to know you and help you find what works for YOU. Coaches and trainers can be expensive, but we all need accountability and support. I'm here to help. With weekly updates, I will be in frequent contact with you to help ensure that you're on the right track. Finding balance and having a healthy mind and body is within reach.

I look forward to joining you on your journey,

alissa

CPSIA information can be obtained
at www.ICGtesting.com
Printed in the USA
LVIC06n1506300817
546748LV00002B/2